$100K BOOK STRATEGY

HOW TO MAKE A 6-FIGURE PASSIVE INCOME
WRITING *"HOW TO"* BOOKS EVEN
IF YOU'RE NOT A WRITER

GRACIE WEIS

© **Copyright Gracie Weis 2022
- All rights reserved**

This book is copyright protected. It is only for personal use. You cannot amend, distribute, sell, use, quote or paraphrase any part of the content without the consent of the author or publisher.

Disclaimer:

Please note that the information contained in this document is for educational and entertainment purposes only. All effort has been executed to present accurate, up-to-date, reliable and complete information. No warranties of any kind are declared or implied.

Readers acknowledge that the author is not engaging in the rendering of legal, financial, medical, or professional advice.

The author makes no guarantees about the results you'll achieve by reading this book. All business requires risk and hard work. Your results may vary when undertaking any new business venture or marketing strategy.

For more information, visit: FreedomMastery.net

Special Bonus Offer

Just to say thank you for purchasing my book, I want to share this Accompanying Business Toolkit for FREE!

Get access to the exact tools, resources, templates & checklists I use every day to grow my publishing business.

It's my gift to you!

Go to https://onebookaway.net/toolkit or scan the bar code below.

Table of Contents

Introduction 1
Who Is This Book For? 5
Why $100K? 9
My Story 11
The Road to $100K 15

Module 1: Building Your Foundation 18
    The Synergized Book Model 18
    Balancing Profitability and Passion 29
    Determining Your Niche's Profitability 32
    Finding the Perfect Niche 38

Module 2: Best Seller Secrets 46
    Positioning Your Book in the Marketplace 46
    How to Develop Your Hook in 3 Easy Steps 48
    Crafting an Irresistible Book Title 52
    Scroll-Stopping Cover Design 57
    Writing a Killer Book Description 60
    Getting Reviews for Your Book 63

Module 3: Creating Books Readers Can't Resist 65
    Making Your Book Unique 65
    Engaging Readers with Your Style 67
    Making Your Content "Readable" 71

Module 4: Pen Names, Book Length & Formatting ... 73
    When to Use a Pen Name 73

How Long Should My Book Be?...75
Formatting and Design..78

Module 5: From Idea to Published 80
Researching Your Topic 82
Brainstorming Chapter Ideas 83
Creating Your "Program" Steps..84
Outlining Each Chapter...87
Creating an Irresistible Table of Contents...........................88

Module 6: Expertly Outsourcing Your Book 91
The Hybrid Ghostwriting Model...92
Hiring Your Ghostwriter..95
Sample Job Post on Upwork..98

Module 7: Keyword and Category Optimization 102
Choosing Your "Big Seven"..105
Identifying Bestseller Categories 108
Advanced Category Strategies 112

Module 8: Building A Raving Fan Base 114
Tracking the Un-trackable...115
Creating a Compelling Lead Magnet....................................117
Setting Up Your Launch Team 121
Running Book Promotions...124
Creating a Killer Author Bio 129

Module 9: The 6-Figure Book Launch Blueprint 133
Why Your Launch Matters...133
My Step-by-Step Launch Strategy..135
    Phase One: Pre-launch...136

Phase Two: Launch Week 137

Phase Three: Post-Launch 138

Keeping Sales Flowing 139

Module 10: Adding Additional Revenue Streams 144

Book Bundle Magic 144

Profiting with Series Pages 147

Double Your Income with Audiobooks............................ 148

Module 11: Selling Your Business For 6-Figures 154

Planning Your Exit Strategy 154

Factors That Determine Business Value 157

When is the Best Time to Sell? 158

Introduction

Welcome to the $100K Book Strategy.

Congratulations on taking the first step towards creating one of the most amazingly passive online businesses that exists today.

I'm really excited to be taking this journey with you!

This book will open your eyes to the incredible opportunity of creating a rewarding and profitable self-publishing business in the growing self-improvement market, *regardless of your writing skills.*

This may sound like a bold statement, and perhaps it is, especially if you've tried self-publishing in the past without having much success. But the reality is, you can go to the Amazon bookstore right now and find dozens of self-publishers in every niche imaginable who are absolutely crushing it using this same exact blueprint.

That said, I want to make it perfectly clear that this is not a get-rich-quick business. It requires commitment, dedication and perseverance on your part to succeed.

So, if you're not afraid of a little hard work to build a better future for yourself, then I invite you to read on!

The Self-Improvement Market is Exploding

It's no secret our world has dramatically changed over the past few years. Because of the economic crisis caused by the pandemic, people around the world have had no choice but to adapt and make changes in multiple areas of their lives.

As a result, people have been flocking to self-improvement bookshelves in greater numbers than ever before in order to keep up with their changing environment.

Whether it's to gain new skills, eat healthier, learn to crochet, make money, build confidence, learn to garden, gain self-esteem, get fit from home, or learn how to create an online business, people are turning to self-improvement books in huge numbers.

The stay-at-home orders mandated by our governments blew the doors wide open for online entrepreneurs. It's no longer limited to only tech-savvy individuals. People who rarely used to purchase products online have become internet shopping junkies. Even many tech-challenged senior citizens have gotten in on the online buying mania.

With online consumption currently at peak levels, the demand for digital content has skyrocketed to the moon. There has literally never been a better time to create an online business in the self-improvement or the self-publishing industry than right now.

And you are about to discover how to reap the rewards from both!

Who Is This Book For?

Entrepreneurs interested in making a positive impact in the world while creating a *scalable, passive income* business and who are looking for the right vehicle to take them there.

Coaches and Course Creators looking to establish authority, credibility, and a steady stream of high-quality targeted leads for their business.

Self-Publishers struggling to scale their business and looking for a successful blueprint to follow.

By *scalable*, I mean the ability to create significant income by producing multiple high-quality books and outsourcing the bulk of the work, including the book creation process itself.

By *passive income,* I mean that as your portfolio of books grow, your royalties will grow in direct proportion and continue to pour into your bank account for years to come - with very little effort on your part!

To get an idea of what scaling to 6-Figures could look like, imagine for a moment that you've just published your first *"how to"* book. And on average, your book sells around 6 copies per day with a profit margin of $4.00 per copy.

It would look something like this:

1 book x 6 sales per day = 6 sales per day

6 books x $4 profit = $24.00 per day

$24 x 30 Days = $720 per month

While $720 per month isn't nearly enough to allow you quit your job yet, it's not bad when you consider that all the hard work you put upfront can pay you for many years to come. That's the beauty of creating this type of semi-passive income.

Now, let's take that a step further. Let's say that over the course of the next ten to twelve months, you publish a total of 12 books that all get similar results.

12 x $720 = $8,640 per month

The above scenario would easily put you on track to earning a 6-figure income. This may be an overly-simplified explanation of the entire process as the number of books to reach 6-figures will vary from publisher-to-publisher depending on a variety of factors that we'll dive into later; but in essence, this is exactly how it works.

Nor could you expect for each of your books to sell a similar number of copies. A more likely scenario is that some books will grossly underperform, a few will wildly overperform and the rest will fall somewhere in between.

But the point I'm trying to make, and the most important thing to remember when it comes to creating success is that *it's <u>not</u> necessary to have a New York Times best-seller or high-profit margins in order to generate a significant income with self-publishing.*

In fact, your highest probability of success is to diversify your sales over multiple books and formats.

This serves two main purposes:

1) It mitigates your overall risk by ensuring that no one book is responsible for your entire revenue. This way, if sales from one of your books suddenly drops off, you don't lose all of your income.

2) It's a heck of a lot easier to sell 1,000 copies from 10 books than it is to sell 10,000 copies from 1 book. The more books you publish, the greater your chances of success.

Right about now you're probably thinking to yourself, *that all sounds great, Gracie, but how in the world am I going to publish multiple books? I'm not even a writer!*

What if I told you that you don't need to be a writer and that you can inexpensively outsource the writing to a professional ghostwriter?

What if all you needed to do was brainstorm good book ideas that help people solve specific problems or achieve certain goals?

How rewarding would it be to know that you're actually building a business where your main objective is helping people improve their lives, while at the same time, you're creating a life of freedom and prosperity for yourself?

From experience, I can tell you that it feels pretty darn amazing. That's why I'm super excited to share this book business model with you. I know the kind of impact it can have on your life and also on the lives of the people you are helping with your books.

So, the real question to ask yourself right now, isn't *if* it's possible to make a significant income with self-publishing, but rather *how* can you do it in the fastest, most efficient, and most profitable way possible.

The answer to that is what this entire book is about.

Why $100K?

At this point, you may be thinking either one of two things:

a) *"$100K? Is that all?" That barely scratches the surface of how much I want to earn.*"

or

b) *"$100K? Are you kidding? At this point, I'd be happy making my first $100 dollars online."*

Regardless of which group you fall into, I think you'll agree that achieving $100K your first year in business is a worthwhile goal, *especially* when it has the potential to generate long-term, semi-passive income.

And while $100K probably won't make anyone *rich*, it can offer something infinitely more important.

Freedom.

The freedom to quit your job and be in charge of your own schedule. The freedom to live life on your own terms. The freedom to make decisions that aren't based in fear or scarcity.

True wealth, in my opinion, is determined by:

- your overall peace of mind.
- the degree of control you feel you have over your life.

- the freedom to pursue the things that are important to you.
- the satisfaction of knowing that you're in charge of your own destiny and that your day-to-day decisions are your own.

With all that being said, there is certainly no reason why you couldn't earn significantly more than 6-figures using the *$100K Book Strategy*. I personally know of a dozen or more self-publishers who are earning upwards of twenty-thousand dollars per month from their book royalties alone.

I know many more who are making two to three times that amount by selling courses and coaching on the backend of their books.

But, as they say, before you can run, you need to learn how to walk. And once you understand the core fundamentals behind creating long-term success with this business model, there are only two things holding you back from creating multiple 6-figures.

Consistency and time.

And of course, publishing more high-quality books aimed at helping people improve their lives. Then, once you have the necessary experience, scaling your revenue is a simple matter of doing *more* of what's already working.

My Story

"We're letting you go, Gracie," the head cook said as she jumped between me and the time clock, blocking me from punching in for my six o'clock bartending shift.

"Excuse me?" I said as I looked at her with what I'm certain was a stupid expression on my face.

"The boss wanted you to have this," she said as she shoved a square white box that was tied with white string at me. She kept her gaze fixed on the box, carefully avoiding any eye contact.

"It's a pie from Cicero's Bakery," she stumbled on. "It's the best bakery in town and *very* expensive. He wanted you to have this. It's apple."

By *"he"*, she meant the owner of the restaurant and bar I worked at. Apparently, *"he"* didn't have the nerve to fire me himself.

I stared down at the box she was holding out, still trying to fully comprehend what she was saying.

A pie? They were firing me and giving me a pie as a consolation prize?

Some employees get watches. Some get severance pay.

I was getting... *a goodbye pie.*

I almost laughed out loud at the thought, but I was too busy trying to hold back my tears.

And to think, it had started out to be such a great day, too. A few hours earlier, I received a call from my mortgage broker, congratulating me on getting approved for our first home loan.

Now what was going to happen? Banks don't give loans to jobless people, do they?

When I got home that night, I remember standing in front of my husband, who was my fiancé at the time, with tears still rolling down my face as I gave him the bad news.

He patiently allowed me to vent, quietly assuring me that everything was going to be okay and we would figure things out. But I could tell by the look on his face he wanted to say something else.

Uh oh, now what? I thought.

He looked down at the box I was still holding, and with a cautious grin asked, *"So...eh...what kind of pie is it?"*

Seriously? Was he kidding? Our future was in shambles and all he could think of was.. *eating pie?*

But I knew him well enough by then to know that he *was* serious. Still, how could I stand by and watch as he enjoyed the pie that symbolized the end of my job and, most probably, our dream of home ownership?

Instead, I made my way over to the trash can and raised the box high above my head, with the intention of slamming it in. But, as I looked back, the sheer panic I saw on his face was so comical that I just couldn't do it.

I burst out laughing instead. We both did. By the time we polished off two-thirds of the pie, my anger and self-pity had been transformed into *sheer determination.*

I made a promise to myself that night that I was going to do everything within my power to prevent anyone or anything from ever having that kind of control over my life again. I was going to start living my life on *my* terms.

And over the course of the next eight years, we went on to build two multiple six-figure businesses, one in the service industry and the other in real estate.

While I can't say everything has always been sunshine and roses or that every business venture I ever tried was a success; I've certainly had my fair share of failures over the years.

But the one thing I can say for sure is *that really was the best damn pie I ever had!*

--- --- ---

I wanted to share this story with you for a couple of reasons. Besides the fact that telling it always gives me chuckle, I'm hoping you recognize that you and I are probably not that much different.

We all have our own adversity and challenges in life that we need to overcome. And sometimes it takes getting knocked to our knees before we're able to summon up the courage to make a real change in our lives. Then it's just a matter of finding the right vehicle to take us to our destination.

You may be reading this book right now because you're in the middle of your own *"goodbye pie"* moment. And perhaps you're searching for the right vehicle that can lead you to the kind of life you always dreamed was possible.

Whatever the reason, just know that you have the power to change things. *You always did.* It may not happen overnight, but it *will* happen if you stay committed and take action. All you need to do is take that first step.

Why not let this book *be* that step?

The Road to $100K

Ever since reading *"The Four-Hour Workweek"* by Tim Ferriss back in 2012, I became obsessed with the idea of owning a different kind of business. One that could offer time freedom, location independence and run without the need for employees.

But was an employee-free, location-independent business really possible?

I didn't know but the idea definitely had me intrigued enough to begin my research.

For almost two years, I bounced around from one online business model to the next, attempting to find one that actually worked the way the gurus claimed it would - an almost impossible task if you know what I mean.

When I was first introduced to the world of self-publishing, I instantly saw the similarities between rental properties and books.

Both were assets capable of earning a high rate of return. Both were capable of producing passive income.

The most obvious advantages with self-publishing are that it requires significantly less startup capital and you won't have to deal with tenants calling you at all hours of the night to repair a clogged toilet.

The more I looked at self-publishing as a business model, the more convinced I became that it had amazing potential. But despite my growing confidence, I hesitated pulling the trigger because I was worried that the industry had become *'too saturated'*.

When you stop to consider how far self-publishing has progressed over the past ten years, you can see how insane my initial fears were.

It made me realize that *"industry saturation"* for the most part, isn't real. It's mostly something we fabricate in our minds so we can avoid doing something that's both scary and new. We use it as our excuse to quit before we ever get started.

Fortunately, I was able to overcome those initial doubts because within a few short months, not only did I earn my initial investment back but I began generating a small profit.

Once I had that proof of concept, I went all in. And within ten months, with the help of ghostwriters and a handful of virtual assistants, those profits grew to just over $10K per month.

And what's even more amazing is that ever since publishing my first book back in 2014, Amazon has been depositing money into my bank account every month, like clockwork.

You may be wondering if it's still possible to have that level of success today just as quickly. The answer is, *absolutely*!

Just recently, I coached a student who had no previous self-publishing experience, launch two low-content books that help dementia patients.

His total investment was $180 to create both books. Not only has he recaptured his original investment, but he's on track to earn $225 to $250 per month in passive income in his third month on two very short books. That's over a 100% return on his investment in less than three months!

There's certainly no doubt that self-publishing platforms have evolved quite a bit over the years due to the high number of spammers and low-quality books being published.

But, in my opinion, it's only made the opportunity much better for those of us who focus on publishing high-quality, value-driven books!

Module 1
Building Your Foundation

"Synergy is what happens when one plus one equals ten or a hundred or even a thousand!" -Steven Covey

The Synergized Book Model

When it comes to creating a successful book publishing business in the self-improvement market, the first step is to understand what makes this business model profitable.

If you don't understand the fundamental differences between self-publishers earning significant royalties versus the ones who are barely scraping by, then you're going to have a difficult time making this model work for you.

The primary goal here isn't to just publish a book or two. The objective is to build a sustainable and profitable business that provides a consistent, passive income, day in and day out.

To accomplish this, you need to adopt the mindset that you're going to dominate whatever niche you choose to go in. It's extremely rare to find a self-publisher earning significant royalties from just one book.

I personally don't know of anyone who is. But I do know quite a few self-publishers who are making a substantial income from multiple books.

So, it's important not to approach this business as if your first book is going to be the *'be-all-end-all'*. Instead, think of your first book as the foundation for all the books that will come after it.

That's why it's essential to create a portfolio of self-improvement books that follow a *Synergized Book Model*.

The *Synergized Book Model* is a method where you focus all your time and effort into serving a single niche, and where each book within that niche, helps to solve a different problem or challenge your audience is having.

At the heart of the Synergized Book Model are two core principles:

1. Multiple books *(launched every 30 to 60 days)*
2. One niche

The concept here is to go as deep as possible into a niche to the point where you have exhausted all ideas and angles for book topics, and there's nothing left for your reader to learn.

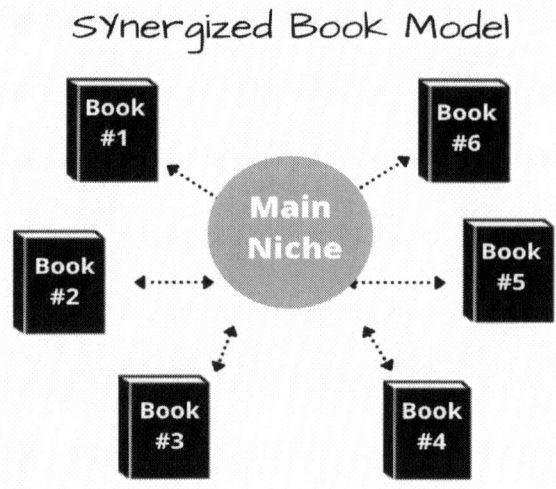

There are a whole host of things at play here that will have a dramatic impact on your results, not to mention drastically reducing your marketing expenses.

One of the biggest mistakes I see many newbie self-publishers make is *niche-hopping*. This is where you jump from one niche to the next, depending on the *hot, new keyword* of the month instead of giving a niche the proper attention and nourishment it needs to grow.

I can tell you from experience that this is a short-term strategy that ultimately leads to unstable book sales. For starters, you never gain any real traction because with every new niche, you are essentially starting from scratch: that includes your audience, marketing and any momentum you gained.

But the real threat actually comes from other self-publishers. It's only a matter of time before your competitors catch wind of your *hot, new keyword* and swoop in to dominate the niche that you didn't. By staking a claim in your niche early, you make it harder for competitors to imitate your success.

It's also vital to remember that audiences of one niche are highly unlikely to cross over into unrelated niches. This is a critical point because it means you won't be able to benefit from the *synergistic* effect of all your previous marketing efforts

Benefits a Synergized Book Model

Increases Customer Read-Through Rate

The *read-through rate (RTR)* is the percentage of people who buy your first book, then go on to buy your other books. The importance of *RTR* on book sales is well-known within the fiction market but still largely ignored in non-fiction circles.

It just makes sense that the more closely related books are in a niche, the greater the chance an audience will read through to your next book.

For example, let's say 1,000 people buy your first book, then 700 of them go on to buy your second book. Your read-through rate from book one to book two is 70%.

Now, let's say that 350 of the 700 customers who bought your second book, go on to read your third book. Your read-through rate from book two to book three is 50%.

So, what does all of this really mean from a money standpoint?

It means that you sold an additional 1,050 books without spending an extra dime on advertising to do it.

Higher Customer Lifetime Value

The *Synergized Book Model* helps you increase your *Customer Lifetime Value (CLV)*. The CLV is the total worth of your customer during the lifetime of your relationship.

Increasing the value of your existing customers is the best way to get a higher return on your investment (ROI), especially when you're running ads. It also allows you to outbid your competitors.

(I apologize in advance for the upcoming math. As painful as it is, it's important that you get an idea of how all of this works.)

For example, let's say you have three books and you price the first book at $2.99 and the other two books at $4.99.

Next, you run an ad campaign for your first book. Soon, the sales start pouring in. Your ad spend costs you approximately 50% of each sale.

That means for every $2.99 book sold, you spend approximately $1.49 in advertising fees. That leaves you with $1.50 in profit, *right?*

Almost. Don't forget that on ebooks priced $2.99 or above, your Amazon royalty is 70% of each sale.

Therefore, it would look more like this:

$2.99 x .70 = $2.09 (minus $1.49 advertising) = $.60

That means your customer lifetime value is $.60 cents. It's not exactly *earth-shattering*, is it? But hold up, this is where your read-through rate comes into play, and things get a bit more exciting.

Using the previous example, if 1,000 people were to buy book #1, and if 700 of those go on to buy book #2, and if 350 of those readers purchase book #3, it ends up looking something like this:

Profit on Book #1: $600.00
Profit on Book #2: $2445.10
Profit on Book #3: $1222.55

Total: $600.00 + $2445.10 + $1222.55 = $4,267.65

You actually end up earning more on books #2 and #3 because there's no advertising expense. So, by simply adding two more books to your series, you increase your total earnings from $600 to $4,267.65.

This boosts your *customer lifetime value* to $4.27 per customer! It may not sound like much, but it can have a huge effect on your bottom line.

Not only does it put more profit in your pocket every time you run advertising to your other books, but it also allows you to bid more competitively.

As you become more advanced, you should aim to increase your customer lifetime value even higher by adding affiliate products or a companion course on the backend of your book funnel. This is how you can double, triple, and even quadruple your revenue.

Positions You as The Authority

A *Synergized Book Model* helps position you as an authority in your niche. Have you ever heard of the three-book rule? It says that if you were to read the top three books on a subject, you would be *perceived as an* expert compared to 99% of the population.

While that may be true, nothing positions you as an expert quite as effectively or as powerfully as actually *writing* a book. This is a generally-accepted fact.

So, what happens when you publish *multiple* books on a topic?

You become the dominant authority.

Positioning yourself as the dominant authority gives you instant mega-credibility. It opens up the doors to serve your audience at even higher levels by offering a course or coaching on the backend. The more potential clients feel like they know, like, and trust you, the easier it is to sell your higher-end products and services.

"Series" Pages

A Synergized Model also enables you to take advantage of *Series Pages*. A series page is a standalone sales page for your books that Amazon creates whenever you link your books together in a *"series"*.

A major advantage of having series pages is higher conversions when running paid ads. Because you are advertising multiple books, you're able to target a range of keywords all at once.

Additionally, because many readers will purchase the full series, your average ticket price can be significantly higher but your ad costs remain essentially the same.

There are a few other benefits to utilizing series pages that are covered in more detail in Module 10. But for now, let's just say that setting up series pages is a very wise move.

Organic Reviews

One of the biggest challenges self-publishers often face is getting organic reviews for their books. *A Synergized Book Model* will help solve your review problem because, by its design, you are continuously building a massive fan base of in-house reviewers.

Multiple books in the same niche helps you to grow your mailing list significantly faster and larger than if you were to have only a single book. Sending periodic emails to a large and loyal fan base can have a substantial effect on the number of reviews your books receive.

When it comes to increasing sales, getting more reviews, and building a stable business, nothing is more important or effective as growing a devoted fan base.

Book Bundles

A *Synergized Book Model* enables you to create multiple book bundles. A book bundle, also known as a boxset, is when you combine two or more books in a related niche to create a completely new *"book"*.

Book bundles are one of the most powerful yet under-utilized ways to exponentially grow your profit margins. They can be a financial windfall for smart self-publishers who understand the benefits.

A book bundle allows you to add an additional revenue stream without the additional time or expense of having to write another book.

You're also able to offer a steep discount to your readers for purchasing multiple books at once, which can significantly increase your sales.

If you're unfamiliar with book bundles or how to create them, they are covered in more detail in Module 10.

Triggers the Amazon Algorithm

If there's one thing you should know about Amazon, it's that they *love* new book releases! In fact, Amazon will even help you market your book for the first thirty days following your launch.

This 30-day launch window opens up the door for you to maximize your visibility, not just for your new release but for all the books within your "funnel".

By intentionally releasing a book every thirty to sixty days (a strategy known as "Rapid Release"), you can consistently capitalize on Amazon's algorithm.

The basic concept behind the rapid release strategy is that the momentum and visibility behind your newly-released books will spill over onto older books, which helps them to consistently stay in front of your target audience.

As they say in the publishing industry, *nothing sells your first book like your second book*. This is just as true for self-publishing.

Powerful Book Launches

The key to launching books successfully is by growing a large, raving fan base. Not only will your fans gobble up your new releases, but they're instrumental with getting those early reviews that are so critical to a book's long-term success.

By following a *Synergized Book Model*, and publishing multiple books in a single niche, you're able to grow a large, targeted audience very quickly.

For example, let's say you publish three books and each one of those attracts 50 email new subscribers each month. That's 150 new subscribers per month.

Within 6 months, you're looking at 900 targeted subscribers to help launch your new books!

Balancing Profitability and Passion

> *"Do what you love and you will never work another day in your life"* - Mark Twain

Choosing the right niche and audience is one of the most important factors that will determine your long-term success and the overall fulfillment you get from your business. Some people find the whole process of choosing a niche tedious and difficult, but it's actually pretty simple.

There's a little bit of science behind finding the perfect niche – it's a mix between market research and finding something you enjoy.

Contrary to what you might have heard, profitability is not the only factor to consider. Too many people make the critical mistake of choosing a niche based purely on income potential.

Now, I'm not arguing that profitability isn't important. Of course, it is. You are in business after all. I'm just saying that it's only half of the equation.

It's equally important to find a niche you're aligned with in some way. Presumably, you are reading this book because you want to build a business that will be successful far into the foreseeable future. And if that's the case, you'll likely be spending a lot of your time working on your business.

So, wouldn't it make sense to choose a niche you actually enjoy, especially when there are literally hundreds of profitable niches to choose from?

By choosing a niche you don't really care about, you make it harder to stay motivated and keep the momentum going long enough to reach success.

In this next section, you're going to learn how to choose a niche that's both profitable *and* gets you excited to jump out of bed in the morning!

The Four Most Profitable Markets

The most profitable self-improvement niches generally fall into one of these four proven, time-tested markets:

- Health
- Wealth
- Relationships
- Passions/hobbies

These markets represent people's core desires. When someone purchases a book in one of these markets, it's because they have a desire to get a certain result in that area of their lives.

When it comes to self-improvement, people don't mind spending a lot of money if they think it will help them achieve a desired outcome. They see it as an investment in themselves.

Within each of one of these main markets are a multitude of ways you can fulfill those desires. These are called submarkets. For example, if you wanted to improve your health, you could do it by:

- losing weight
- managing your diabetes
- eating healthier
- gaining muscle mass

Similarly, if you're seeking wealth, you could choose to do it through:

- real estate
- stocks
- cryptocurrencies
- online marketing

Each one of these subcategories can be further broken down into even more specific ways to fulfill those desires. These are called niches.

Here's what it looks like:

Core Market—>Subcategory—>Niche

Health—>Nutrition—>Raw Diet
Health —>Weight Loss—>Ketogenic Diet

Wealth—>Investing—>Bit currencies
Wealth—>Real Estate —>Flipping Mobile Homes

Relationships—>Marriage—>How to Stay in Love
Relationships—>Parenting—>Homeschooling Teenagers

Hobbies—>Photography—>Landscape Photography
Hobbies—>Gardening—>Square Foot Gardening

These examples barely scratch the surface of what's available. As you start looking around, you'll come across niches you never even dreamed existed.

Start thinking about some of the things that you enjoy. Do they fall within one of these four core markets? Once you find a few niches that you resonate with, your next step is to investigate the potential profitability of your idea.

Determining Your Niche's Profitability

One of the fastest and easiest ways to know if your niche is profitable is to do research to see if there are any courses or coaching being offered on the topic. If you find a lot of courses being sold, it's a good indication that the niche has high profitability potential and it deserves further examination.

Many people see competitive niches as something to be avoided, but that's really the wrong way to think about it. Competition is actually a good thing. If other people are making money in a certain niche, then it's a major opportunity to take something that's already been proven to work and throw your own spin on it.

Remember, your job isn't to reinvent the wheel; create a better one.

Begin by doing a quick search on websites like Clickbank, Udemy, and Teachable to see how many courses are available on your topic. Take the time to understand the kinds of courses being offered and research the following:

- What topics do they cover?
- What's their angle?
- How many reviews do they have? A niche with a lot of reviews clues you in on its popularity.
- What do reviewers love about the course?
- What are reviewers complaining about?

Comments are by far my favorite way to get a more in-depth look at who my customers are and what kind of challenges they are struggling with.

Validating Your Niches Profitability

There are a number of ways gurus recommend validating your niche's profitability; but in my opinion, most are a waste of time.

If Amazon is the platform where you intend to publish your first book, which is what I recommend, then it makes sense to start your due diligence there.

Amazon is, after all, the biggest retailer of books. When someone is actively searching on Amazon, it usually means they intend to make a purchase. As you begin to do your research, here are some questions to ask yourself:

- *Are people already actively searching for your book idea?*
- *Are there similar books in your niche?*
- *Are those books making sales?*
- *How competitive is the market?*

Naturally, the most profitable niches will be the ones selling the most books. To determine how well a book is selling on Amazon, all you need to do is look for the BSR number found on the book's product page.

The BSR, which stands for Best Sellers Rank, is a number Amazon assigns to books once they have made at least one sale.

The lower the BSR number, the higher the volume of books being sold. Conversely, the higher the BSR number, the lower the volume of books being sold.

A book with a BSR ranking of #1 is the best-selling book on all of Amazon. A book with a BSR ranking of #100 is the 100th best-selling book.

For example:

#100 BSR = 300 sales per day
#1000 BSR = 72 sales per day
#10,000 BSR = 12 sales per day

#50,000 BSR = 3 sales per day
#100,000 BSR = 1 sale per day

These are just examples of book sales according to Amazon as of today, but these numbers are always changing. To find a book's BSR, scroll down the book's product page. The best sellers rank will be listed under *Product Details*.

Product details
ASIN : B08L6VQZMG
Publication date : October 13, 2020
Language : English
File size : 627 KB
Simultaneous device usage : Unlimited
Text-to-Speech : Enabled
Enhanced typesetting : Enabled
X-Ray : Not Enabled
Word Wise : Enabled
Print length : 150 pages
Page numbers source ISBN : B08L3Z2THC
Lending : Enabled
Best Sellers Rank: #175,139 in Kindle Store (See Top 100 in Kindle Store)
   #163 in Time Management in Business
   #450 in Personal Time Management
   #3,306 in Success Self-Help
Customer Reviews: ★★★★☆ 11 ratings

Keep in mind that BSRs fluctuate up or down, depending upon the day of the week and time of day. For example, one of my books sells the most copies on Wednesdays, and the BSR is usually at its lowest on that day.

If you want to get a more accurate assessment of how many sales a book is making, you can go to Kindlepreneur.com and type "calculator" into the search bar.

Another free tool I highly recommend is DS Amazon Quickview. This is a Google Chrome extension that lets you quickly view product details and BSR ranking. It will save you a ton of time when doing your competitor research.

Finding Profitable Keywords on Amazon

Before you get started searching for profitable keywords, make sure you are using Google's incognito mode to prevent your previous searches from affecting the results.

1. To open in incognito mode, click the three dots located at the upper right on your Google browser.

2. Next, go to the Amazon book store and start typing in your top keywords for your niche in the search bar. As you begin typing, Amazon will pre-populate with a dropdown of the **10** most searched keywords in the search box.

THE $100K BOOK STRATEGY

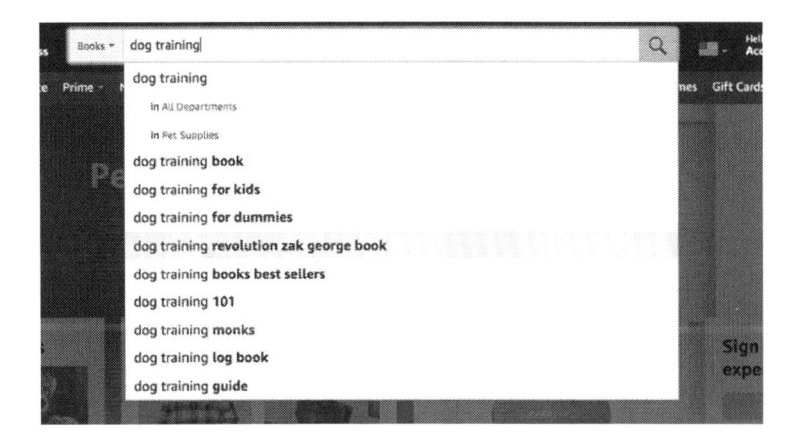

![Amazon search dropdown showing dog training keyword suggestions]

You can expand Amazon's keyword suggestions even further by installing another free Google Chrome app, AMZ Suggestion Expander.

This will give you even more variations of keywords that people are using to search for a product.

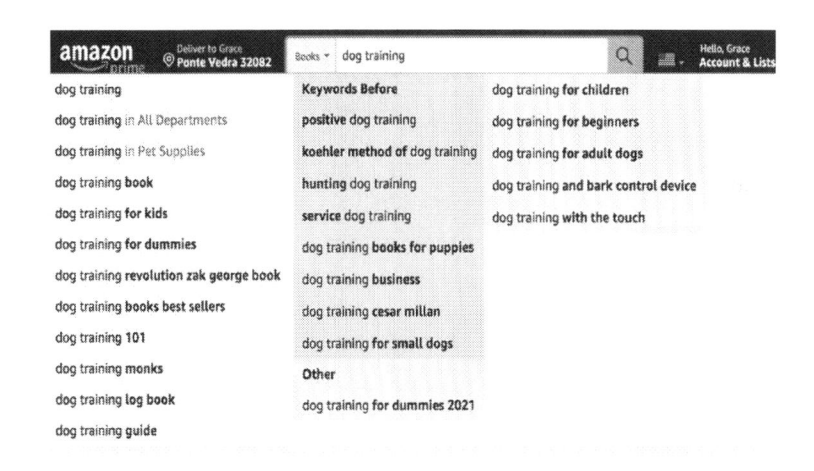

![AMZ Suggestion Expander results for dog training]

3. Next, record all the keywords that correspond to your book idea.

4. Then, copy and paste each keyword in the search bar. Now, count how many books have BSRs less than 50,000 on the first page.

If Amazon doesn't return any suggestions or returns less than 10 results, it's a good indication there is a low demand for your book idea or niche.

The more books you find on the first page with very low BSRs, the higher the demand will be for that keyword. It usually means higher competition as well.

As a rule of thumb, I like to see at least three books with BSRs below 50,000 on the first page. If there are less than three, it usually indicates there probably isn't enough demand for that keyword.

The BSR method may not always be the most precise tool for calculating sales and profitability, but it can give you a decent guess-estimate.

Finding the Perfect Niche

Now that you understand that there are literally hundreds of profitable markets to choose from, it's time to find one you align with on a personal level.

As discussed earlier, choosing your niche is not only an opportunity to make money; it's also a chance to do something that you enjoy and adds a sense of fulfillment to your life.

In many ways, finding your perfect niche can be compared to the Japanese concept of *Ikigai*.

The word *Ikigai* translates to *your purpose or your reason for getting out of bed in the morning.*

According to the Japanese, your *Ikigai* is finding the intersection between:

- What you love
- What you are good at
- What the world needs
- What you can get paid for

[Venn diagram showing four overlapping circles: WHAT YOU LOVE, WHAT YOU ARE GOOD AT, WHAT THE WORLD NEEDS, WHAT YOU CAN BE PAID FOR, with intersections labeled Passion, Mission, Profession, Vocation, and Ikigai at the center]

Many of us fall into the trap of believing that the pursuit of money and doing work we enjoy are on opposite sides of the same coin.

On one side, we all want to live a certain lifestyle that money can buy. On the other side, we want to live a life of purpose and fulfillment. We don't feel like we can have both.

But nothing could be further from the truth. In fact, achieving success is a thousand times easier when you're serving a niche you actually enjoy.

Once you take the time to discover a niche you naturally align with, the self-publishing platform is the perfect medium for expressing that passion. To help you uncover your ideal niche, ask yourself the following questions:

Are You Passionate About the Topic?

Do you really need to be "passionate" about your niche? I think the whole "find your passion" thing can be very confusing for people which will prevent them from ever moving ahead. That's why so many people stay "stuck" when choosing a niche.

A confused mind will never take action.

Finding your passion can be simpler than you think and not some life-long quest. The degree of passion we have for anything usually correlates with how competent we feel about doing a certain thing.

That's all passion is, really. We do something we like and get better at it; the better we get, the more we like it. It doesn't have to be anything more complicated than that.

So, if you truly want to be effective in your niche so that you can help people, you need to find something you enjoy enough to want to get better at.

Writing quality self-improvement books and building an audience takes time, money and commitment. The real magic doesn't begin to happen sometimes until you publish your 2nd or 3rd book.

When you choose a niche that you don't have any interest beyond the potential financial gain, it becomes easier to quit when things don't go as planned. Having a purely financial goal won't be enough to drag you across the finish line when doubt begins to creep in.

After finding some potential niches that interest you, ask yourself the following:

- Is this a niche I'd like to master?
- Is this a niche I would pursue even if I don't get paid?
- Do I find myself researching this niche in my spare time?
- Can I see myself being in this niche a year or longer down the road?

If you can't imagine yourself publishing multiple books, doing hours of research on the topic, building a social media fanbase or offering related products or courses, then it's probably not the right niche for you.

Does Your Niche Already Have a Passionate Audience?

Are there Facebook groups, YouTube channels, and blogs dedicated to your niche? Are gurus offering coaching or selling courses in this niche?

The more passionate an audience is about a topic, the more they will have an unquenchable thirst for knowledge. Audiences that are "irrationally exuberant" about a topic are continuously hunting down new content to improve themselves or their skill sets.

These are by far the _best_ kinds of niches to be in; the ones that audiences care deeply about.

More Passion = More Profits

Below are a few passionate niches that have a huge appetite for content:

- Law of attraction
- Mindset
- Motivation
- Traveling
- Making money
- Saving money

- Productivity
- Female entrepreneurs
- Online marketing
- Parenting
- Real estate
- Investing
- Dating

These are high-information, evergreen niches that do well in all economies: recessions, depressions or booms.

Does Your Niche Have Multiple Problems to Solve?

This is key. Your niche needs to be broad enough to accommodate a series of books. Remember, your first book is your starting point, not the end game. Your goal isn't to have just one bestselling book, but to have several.

For that reason, you want to choose a niche with multiple problems to solve or one that is continuously seeking knowledge to improve their understanding.

For example, entrepreneurs in the online marketing niche are always searching out information on e-mail marketing, webinars, Facebook marketing, YouTube marketing, etc.

Likewise, real estate investors have an unquenchable thirst for information regarding lease options, flipping, rehabbing, wholesaling, land-lording, foreclosures, tax auctions, etc. There are numerous topics to choose from.

Avoid niches that only have one problem or challenge to solve. For instance, some people are passionate about Labradoodles, but it would be difficult to publish multiple books on this topic.

It's unlikely to be profitable beyond just one or two books because there aren't enough sub-niches to expand on.

What areas can you share in which you possess knowledge, talent, or experience?

If possible, always choose a niche where you can share your personal knowledge or expertise. Not only can you share your story in your book, but you'll also be able to relate to your audience and better understand their frustrations.

The best niches are ones where you feel like you are part of the target audience already.

Take some time to think about some of the problems you were personally able to overcome. You didn't get through life without learning a few things along the way.

Perhaps you're good at organizing spaces or were able to lose a lot of weight. Maybe you're good at homeschooling your kids or you were able to pay off all your debt quickly.

Your expertise probably won't feel like an earth-shattering achievement and chances are, you're probably overlooking its value.

But there are still millions of people in the world still struggling to do what you were able to overcome. They're just waiting for you to step up and share it in a way that only you can.

Module 2
Best Seller Secrets

"Marketing begins before the product is ever launched." -Seth Godin

Positioning Your Book in the Marketplace

Now that you've chosen a niche, it's time to start thinking about how you're going to position and market your book. If you wait until your book is published before deciding how to market it, it may already be too late.

Marketing your book doesn't begin after you push the publish button. It begins the very moment the idea for your book is born.

One of the most important sales decisions you can ever make is knowing how you're going to optimize your book right from the start.

The time and effort you spend in these early stages can pay big dividends well into the future, so it's worth getting this one right.

Hook, Line & Sales

Before you put one word to paper, you need to de
the *hook* for your book. Essentially, a book hook is a brief synopsis of your book's core concept written in a way that appeals to your target audience. Said in another way, it's your book's *angle*.

A good book hook contains a unique feature that will set your self-help or *"how-to"* book apart from all the other books in your niche. Identifying your hook early on will help you to map out your book's content and keep your messaging crystal clear.

One of the most important questions your hook needs to answer is: *how is your method of solving the problem unique, and what differentiates your book from all the others on the self-improvement bookshelves?*

No one wants to read a rehash of a book they've already read before. Readers want fresh ideas and new perspectives. If you see readers leaving comments like *"nothing new here"* or *"read it all before"*, it's a pretty good sign that the book has a weak hook.

A book that fails to appeal to its target audience can rarely be saved regardless of how many advertising dollars are spent.

It's also imperative that your book answers the reader's question, *"what's in it for me?"* The answer to that question should be the prominent message of your book, especially the book's title and description.

Let's face it, people aren't going to buy your book just because you have a sexy author bio. The only thing they care about is how your book can improve their current situation.

Developing Your Hook in 3 Easy Steps

The most important thing to remember when developing a hook for your self-improvement book is that people don't buy tactics.

They buy processes and systems.

Tactics are a dime a dozen. No one wants to buy information that can be found on the internet with a five-second Google search. People want a replicable process that can be followed to achieve a specific result.

People don't mind spending money for information when it's presented as a system or framework designed to help them achieve a desired outcome.

For example, consider a book titled, "*20 Ways to Lose Weight Fast"* or "*75 Tips to Become Debt-free.*" Both of these titles describe *tactics*. They sound like they should be long blog posts rather than books that provide specific solutions to problems.

Compare those to the following titles:

"*The Green Juice Diet: Drop Fat & Blast Through Plateaus Drinking Healthy Green Juice*"

or

"*Debt-Free Life: How I Paid Off $100K in Consumer Debt in Just 12 Months.*"

Both of these book titles offer the promise of a unique solution. Although not outwardly stated, they imply the book contains a specific plan or process the reader can follow to achieve a specific result.

When information is presented in a random way, it only causes more confusion and chaos in the mind of the reader. Do you really want to be the one who *adds* to the chaos by offering *101 ways* of doing something?

Why not make your readers happy by giving them what they want? An easy solution or simple method that helps them solve a particular problem.

Bonus points if your reader hasn't tried or heard of this solution in the past.

When you understand the challenges your reader is experiencing at a core level, creating your book hook is a straightforward process that can be accomplished in 3 simple steps.

Step #1: Identify your audience's problem.

Step #2: Form the problem into a question.

Step #3: Position your book as the unique, simplified solution.

For example, let's say you have a book that shows people how they can raise their credit scores.

Problem: People who want to increase a low credit score.

Question: Is your low credit score hurting your chances of buying a home or car?

Solution*:* Learn the exact strategies and techniques to increase your credit score by 100+ points in as little as 90 days.

Say your book is about attraction marketing*:*

Problem: Small business owners who hate prospecting.

Question*:* Would you like to double your revenue but hate prospecting for new clients?

Solution: Learn how the Attraction Sales Method will have clients lining up to do business with you, ready to buy whatever you have to offer without ever doing cold reach.

Notice these examples are very specific as to what the reader can expect to learn from the book. In today's competitive market, you can't afford to be vague. Your message needs to cut through all the crap.

The questions below will help you get granular so you can identify your hook:

- What problem are your readers trying to solve?
- Who is your ideal reader and what result do they want to achieve?
- What is the promise of your book and does your book keep that promise?
- Does your book have a strategy or process that solves your reader's problem?
- What makes your book unique? What can your book offer that no other book does? (It can be as simple as how your book is presented or structured.)
- What makes you angry or frustrates you at how other books are presented? How do you think it should be written?

Finding your hook can take a little creativity on your part. Don't worry too much if it doesn't come to you right away. Be patient. The best ideas often come when you least expect them.

Crafting an Irresistible Book Title

The impact your book title and subtitle has on your sales cannot be overstated. Good titles have the power to turn casual browsers into excited buyers. Bad titles have the power to permanently bury your book in obscurity.

Apart from the book cover, the title is the first thing a potential reader considers when deciding whether or not to purchase a book. It's your earliest opportunity to market your book and stake your claim in a niche.

But creating a great book title can be a bit tricky. It's a balancing act between capturing your audience's attention, explaining what your book is about and showcasing the benefits in as few words as possible.

Irresistible Titles Grab Attention

Every day our brains are bombarded with more information than our brains can possibly process, most of which has no relevance to our daily lives.

Fortunately for us, we come pre-programmed with a reticular activating system (RAS) in our brains that enables us to quickly weed out all the "useless information".

That's why it's crucial that your book title grabs your reader's attention within the first five seconds; otherwise, you risk becoming *invisible*.

So how do you grab your reader's attention long enough to bypass these *useless information* filters?

- Use "buzzwords" that your ideal reader's subconscious brain will immediately pick-up.

- Make your ideal readers curious. Curiosity is a powerful way to capture attention.

- Titles that are *controversial, go against the norm* or *make grand promises* can compel a reader to take notice, even when they're not paying attention.

A great example of this is *"The Four-Hour Workweek"* by Tim Ferriss. The title invokes both intrigue and curiosity. We may have an idea of what the book's about, but we don't *really* know. It almost *forces* us to investigate it further.

The promise (lure) of a four-hour workweek is very compelling, especially for people who work long hours or really hate their jobs. The title piques our curiosity by defying conventional wisdom.

Here are some other honorable mentions that also do an amazing job.

- *"The 12 Week Year: Get More Done in 12 Weeks than Others Do in 12 Months by Brian Moran (goes against the norm)*

- *"The Motivation Myth: How High Achievers Really Set Themselves Up to Win"* by Jeff Haden (controversial)

- *"The Laptop Millionaire: How Anyone Can Escape the 9-5 and Make Money Online"* by Mark Anastasi (grand promise)

Irresistible Titles Are Descriptive

People searching for information don't read. They scan. Modern life is busy, and people don't want to waste time trying to figure out what your book is about. A title needs to convey to your audience in a few words or short phrases (including the subtitle) what your book is about and how it can help them achieve their desired result.

Make sure to use words or phrases that are immediately understandable by your target audience. Words that have meaning to your reader will auto-trigger their brains to pay attention.

Irresistible Titles Are Short

Yes, size matters, especially when it comes to your book title. Most potential readers will first encounter your book at thumbnail size. If you don't want readers to quickly swipe past, then make sure your title is visible at a small scale. Remember, the shorter the title, the larger the font. Conversely, the longer the title, the less readability.

According to Amazon's top 100 bestseller list, the ideal title contains four to six words or less. Personally, I always try to shoot for three to four words for my main title. It's short enough to create curiosity and long enough to hint at what the book is about.

Keep in mind that Amazon mobile only shows about twenty characters of your title beneath the thumbnail. The rest gets cut off.

Tying it all Together

Next, you want to follow up your main title with a longer, explanatory, and keyword-rich subtitle. Ideally, your subtitle will contain your *hook* as discussed in the previous section.

Think of it like this: Your main title is the lure that attracts readers' eyeballs and your subtitle is the hook that reels them in.

To illustrate all the above steps, let's break down how I came up with the title for this book:

"*$100K*" indicates that the book is about making money. I thought about the result my target audience wants to achieve. I know from reading through hundreds of comments on social media that most self-publishers have a goal to make $100K. It was also my goal when I first got started with self-publishing.

I also wanted to distinguish this book from others in the niche that focus on *how to publish* a *bestseller*. Those titles tend to attract mainly authors whose primary goal is attaining a certain status rather than creating a business. Plus, I didn't want to alienate entrepreneurs who don't consider themselves "*authors*".

"*Book*" hints at the *how* or the modality for achieving the result. It lets my audience know that this book pertains to them.

"*Strategy*" lets readers know that the book contains a system or framework they can follow. Remember, potential readers are looking for solutions, not tactics.

It's okay if your title doesn't come to you right away: it's a creative process. Most times, it will come when you least expect it. My best ideas usually happen when I'm running or in the shower.

Other great titles for inspiration:

"*Total Money Makeover: A Proven Plan for Financial Fitness*" by Dave Ramsey

"*The Gifts of Imperfection: Let Go of Who You Think You're Supposed to Be and Embrace Who You Are*" by Brené Brown

"Profit First: Transform Your Business from a Cash Eating Monster to a Money-Making Machine" by Michalowicz

"Born to Win: Find Your Success Code" by Zig Ziglar

If you're feeling stuck and need more inspiration, check out Amazon's current best sellers list.

Scroll-Stopping Cover Design

Besides your book's title, your cover has the biggest impact on marketing. It may be cliché, but people absolutely do judge books by their covers.

Your book cover has one job to do: capture attention so potential readers don't scroll past. It also needs to convey what your book is about in five seconds or less.

I've found that the best covers tend to be simple and minimalistic. Sometimes less is just more. Background images and crazy fonts can be a big distraction from the overall message of a book. If your book title and book hook are effective, most times you don't need much more.

At minimum, the best covers will usually have these five elements:

1. *A Prominent Title.* Your title should be the main focal point of the book cover.

2. *Font Style.* A style that's easy to read. Avoid those gimmicky fonts that make so many self-published books look amateurish.
3. *Font Size.* A size that's easy to read at thumbnail size. The bigger the better.
4. *Simple Design.* The graphics need to complement the title, not compete against it. Don't let your design get in the way of your cover's readability.
5. *Contrast.* Choose the right background and font colors that grab attention. Darker font colors on a white/light background (my favorite) can make a book pop off the page.

Do You Need an Expensive Cover Designer?

Some gurus recommend it, but I don't feel like it's always necessary, especially if you're just starting out and funds are tight. There's no guarantee that hiring an expensive cover designer will make your book a bestseller.

I know many authors who have spent thousands of dollars on book covers only to have their books flop. It's not the cost of the cover that makes the difference. It's how well the cover captures the reader's attention and how professional it appears.

One thing I strongly advise against is creating your own book covers unless you're a skilled graphic designer or artist. Why risk the success of your book when you can get a professional cover made for less than thirty dollars on Fiverr?

In order to get the best results from designers on Fiverr, I recommend:

1. Only work with the highest-rated designers (Level 2 or Top-Rated Sellers).

2. Brainstorm your own book cover concepts. I tend to get the best results when I give the designer a clear vision of my cover concept. I usually provide a rough mock-up of my idea that I create on Canva. This gives them a better understanding of my vision so they aren't shooting completely in the dark.

The best way to find inspiration for your book covers is by browsing other non-fiction bestsellers on Amazon. Don't limit yourself to browsing only in your niche. Expanding your search into other categories will give you a broad range of ideas and will help to stimulate your creative side.

The last thing you want is for your cover to end up looking like everyone else's. Your number one objective is to stand out from the competition.

Here are some questions to ask yourself when browsing the bestsellers list:

- Which book covers grab my attention?

What feature makes them stand out?

What colors and contrasting are they using?

- What kind of images or backgrounds are they using?
- How can I make a similar design idea work for my niche?

If you have the funds and would rather have a graphic designer create both your cover concept and overall design, I recommend going with 99Designs.com. They are more expensive, but they offer multiple high-quality design concepts from top-notch designers. Prices can range from $199 to $1,199 depending upon how many designs you want and the designer's skill level.

But if it's not in the budget at the moment, don't sweat it. A major advantage to self-publishing is that you can easily update your book at a later date.

Writing a Killer Book Description

The book description, while not quite as important as your title or book cover, plays an important role when it comes to sales.

Despite what many people think, the purpose of a book description *isn't* to provide a summary of your entire book. It's your marketing pitch to potential readers.

A good description has three main objectives.

- to tease and entice readers to pick up your book
- to persuade readers that your book offers a unique solution to their problem
- to convey a clear promise of what they will gain by reading it.

Now that you know what a good book description is *supposed* to do, here are the steps for *how* to do it.

Create a Compelling Headline. The first line of your description needs to grab the reader's attention. The Amazon product page only displays the first few lines of your book description. That leaves you with a very small window of opportunity to capture a reader's attention.

Most readers won't take the time to click on the "read more" button if the first sentence doesn't pique their interest. One way to grab attention is by starting your headline with a question or statement that summarizes the result or transformation the reader is seeking. For example:

"Would You Like to Discover the Secrets to Getting a Lean, Sexy Waistline with Zero Exercise?"

"What if There Was a Way You Could Manifest Your Dream Partner by Using Simple Law of Attraction Techniques?"

"Learn the Secrets of How I Raised My Credit Score 100 Points with These 5 Easy Steps."

Describe the Problem/Pain. Once you have their attention, the next step is to describe the current pain they're experiencing in simple, everyday language. Readers need to believe you understand their pain.

Describe How Your Book Will Solve Their Problem. Tell readers how your book offers the solution to their pain or problem. Remember, they will only buy your book if they believe it will help them achieve a desired result.

Make it Keyword Rich. Your description should contain various keywords related to the book's topic so that Amazon's algorithm is triggered to show your book whenever readers perform a search. This does not mean you should keyword stuff. Keyword stuffing doesn't do anything but flag your book as low quality.

Keep it Short. Most bestsellers have descriptions less than 200 to 250 words long. Keep it short and to the point. Don't let your description ramble.

Make it scannable. Make your description easy for readers to scan by using two or three short sentences per paragraph. Avoid using block text.

Use Bullet points. Add 5-7 short bullet points that briefly describe what they will learn in your book. These bullet points should be written in a way that triggers curiosity. For example: *In this book, you'll learn the 3 secrets that will raise your credit score by 50 points in 7 days.*

Add Testimonials. Add a few powerful testimonials to your description from customers who have previously reviewed your book. If you don't have reviews at this point, you can always go back and add them later.

Getting Reviews for Your Book

Many readers rely on social validation to confirm whether a book is worth reading. The more positive reviews a book has, the more proof the book is a good purchase.

Despite what many people think, reviews don't directly impact a book's sales rank. Sales rank is mostly determined by the number of sales and downloads a book gets, not by the number of positive or negative reviews.

What reviews do heavily impact is the conversion rate. Books with a lot of positive reviews are highly effective at converting browsers into buyers. The higher your conversion rate, the higher your sales rank. It's a subtle difference but one worth pointing out.

You may not think you have any control over how many reviews your book gets, but you do. In Module 8, you'll learn some specific methods for accumulating dozens of reviews following your book's release.

But for now, the simplest but most overlooked strategy for getting reviews is to simply *ask* for them.

Include a clear call to action at the end of your book, like this:

"If you liked this book, could you please do me a favor and leave a review? Your words will help share my message with the people who may need it the most.

Your support is greatly appreciated.

*Click here to leave a review:
https://www.amazon.com/review/create-review?asin=XXXXXXXX*

That's it! You'd be surprised at how effective simply asking can be. It's also super important to make it easy for readers to leave you a review by giving them a link to your Amazon review page.

Simply replace the X's with your book's ASIN number and it will take readers directly to your book's review page.

As business coach, Sam Ovens says, "You need to eat your customer's complexity.[1]

In other words, if you want your customer to do something, then you need to remove any obstacles blocking their path.

Module 3
Creating Books Readers Can't Resist

"Everything that needs to be said has already been said. But since no one was listening, everything must be said again." -André Gide

Making Your Book Unique

If you want thousands of readers lining up to read your books, join your Facebook group, and hop onto your e-mail list, then you need to start by publishing books that readers actually want to read.

But what if there are already multiple books written on my topic?

Your topic doesn't need to be original. In fact, there's a 99% chance that it won't be. What *is* important is that your ideas are presented with a new and fresh perspective.

Some topics have been around for hundreds of years but has that ever stopped anyone from rewriting them with fresh viewpoints and new writing styles? *No way!*

Readers are always looking for new and different ways to solve a problem or improve a skill. There could be hundreds of books on the topic, but none of them will have your unique process or way of doing things. *That's what will set your book apart from the rest.*

Look at motivational speakers, for example. They have been recycling the same ideas for hundreds of years, yet we never seem to grow tired of them.

Why is that?

Because each speaker has adopted their own style and twist on how they present old ideas. It's not that they're saying anything new; they're just presenting the information in a way that's unique to them.

> *Facts and statistics alone don't make a book worth reading.*

It's the author's views and personality injected into a book that make it really interesting. *For example*, this book is the combination of my own life experience plus dozens of books I've read and courses I've taken over the years. Writing a book on how to make money writing a book is far from a new concept.

But it's my perspective, my style of writing, my unique process, and the way that I've structured the book that makes it unique.

Engaging Readers with Your Style

Writing style can have a very profound effect on the connections you build with your audience. One powerful and effective way to engage your audience is by writing in a conversational tone.

Conversational writing makes an author seem more relatable and the content far more interesting because readers are able to see there's actually a real person behind all the words.

Just because self-improvement books are meant to be informational doesn't mean they should read like a college text book.

The problem is that many non-fiction authors have a tendency of writing very formally, as if they're addressing a room full of faculty members instead of chatting with a friend over coffee.

Formal writing can come across as impersonal or unfeeling, and is very different from how we actually talk in everyday life.

There was an interesting experiment conducted by Neil Patel, co-founder of Kissmetrics.com[2], where he split-tested two versions of his blog introduction-one written in a conversational tone and the other in a formal tone.

The results of the test were pretty astounding. A whopping 247% more readers went on to read the full blog post that was written in the conversational tone. Readers also stayed on his page for an additional 3:20 minutes longer.

The outcome provides strong evidence that as readers, we don't want to be lectured, we want to be engaged.

Tips for Writing Conversationally

Write to an Audience of One

Write as if you're writing to one reader instead of speaking to thousands of nameless, faceless strangers. Address your readers by using "*you*". It makes readers feel as if you're writing to them personally.

Try to write as if you're sharing your ideas with a friend or co-worker who's asked for your advice. For example, "The best way to train a dog is with positive reinforcement" vs "The best way for *you* to train *your* dog is to give him positive reinforcement."

See the difference?

Write in the present tense

Don't write in the future tense; be in the moment. For example, don't say, "*before* writing your book, you *will* need to research keywords on Amazon." Instead say, "*go to Amazon's search bar and type in your keyword.*" It makes readers feel that you are right there with them.

Keep Paragraphs Short

At the heart of conversational writing is readability. Shorter paragraphs keep your readers' attention and make your writing more inviting. Long, blocky paragraphs are tough to read and a turn-off to readers. By keeping your paragraphs short, you ensure that your message is easy to understand and to the point.

Ask Questions

Asking questions is a great way to keep your writing style conversational. Questions engage the reader directly and give them something to think about. It keeps them in the conversation and makes the reading experience more interactive and personalized.

Makes sense, right?

Just make sure you follow up your questions with the answers, so you don't leave your reader hanging.

Use Contractions

We use contractions in everyday conversation, so why not use them in your writing? Forget what you learned in grade school. We live in the era of "text speak".

Contractions help convey a friendly and less formal tone that readers understand and can relate to. Example: *"I cannot do that"* vs *"I can't do that."*

Write Short Sentences

Keep your sentences short: they're easier to read and digest. Longer sentences require more effort to process. Try breaking longer sentences into several shorter ones to make them more readable.

Choose Simple Words

Avoid using words you wouldn't use in a real conversation. For example, if your friend enjoys playing tennis you wouldn't say, "Amy is quite the *fitness enthusiast*." The only people who use that term in real life are health and fitness writers.

Add Some Personality

Don't be afraid to inject some of your own personality into your writing; it will make your content seem far more interesting. Use common phrases as if you are talking with a friend. It helps to create a better connection with your readers.

Remember, you're establishing yourself as a unique authority in your niche. Your personality, unique tone and voice need to stand out. When you're able to do this in an authentic and professional way, readers will instantly connect with your content.

If you're not writing the book yourself, forward this list to your ghostwriter so they understand what you mean by a conversational writing style.

Make Your Content *"Readable"*

Many authors don't realize the overall impact that readability has on a book's *likeability*. Readers don't want to work hard to consume your content.

Reading should be an enjoyable activity. Using large blocks of text, small fonts, and difficult-to-read fonts irritate readers. The last thing you want is for them to struggle getting through your content.

Whenever I see large blocks of text or small fonts that strain my eyes, most times I will skip right over the content, *even if the information is good.* It's just not something my brain wants to tackle.

Consider for a moment that most adults over the age of forty have some type of vision problem. You could end up alienating a significant portion of your readers. If your goal really is to help people overcome problems and challenges that they're facing, then why not start by helping them overcome the challenge of reading your book?

Tips for improving readability:

- Use easy-to-read fonts (Georgia, Helvetica, Verdana, Arial, Tahoma, Georgia, Times Roman).

- Write at a 7th or 8th-grade level. The average adult reads at the 9th-grade level. If you want to write something readers can easily comprehend and enjoy, write 1 to 2 grades below their actual reading grade level.

- Limit your paragraphs to just a few sentences and avoid big blocks of hard-to-read text.

- Use subheadings and **bold** to call attention to important information and help break up the text between chapters.

- Use bullet points to organize and break up text.

- Add pictures, infographics, and graphs to make your content more interesting. It also helps readers with a strong visual modality for learning. This is especially true for self-help and *how-to* books.

- Don't use less than an 11-point font for printed books.

- Use 1.15 line spacing for easier reading.

Module 4
Pen Names, Book Length and Formatting

When to Use a Pen Name

One of the most frequent questions people have when they first get started is whether to use a pen name or not. The honest answer is that it really depends upon your long-term goals.

For fiction writers, using a pen name is a commonly accepted practice and pretty much the norm. But for non-fiction writers, it can be a bit trickier.

For starters, a pen name can make marketing your personal brand more difficult. Keep in mind that you'll need to take on that pen name persona in your e-mails, advertising, social media accounts, and any course on the backend, should you decide to create one.

It can also be hard to connect with your audience if you're not being your *"real"* self. Not only does it feel disingenuous, but it also puts you at risk of losing reader trust and credibility if people discover you're not using your real name. You will also lose a certain level of fulfillment you get that comes with connecting with your readers on a personal level.

On the flip side, there are some legitimately good reasons why you may want to use a pen name.

- If your long-term goal is to sell your publishing business at some point, using a pen name makes a lot of sense.

- If you're someone who is totally happy staying "behind the scenes".

- If you are building multiple brands in totally unrelated niches and want to avoid being perceived as a *"jack of all trades"* instead of an expert of one.

  For example, how would you feel if Dave Ramsey, who's famous for giving financial advice, all of sudden started giving you fitness advice? It would feel kind of weird and probably wouldn't go over so well.

One way to navigate around these credibility issues and the feeling of *"fake"* marketing is to publish your books under a publishing company name.

There are quite a few successful self-publishers who are making a significant income without using a pen name at all. By publishing all their books under their publishing company name, they're able to run their business completely independent from their personal brand. It also allows them to cross-promote other books in related niches to their email list.

On the other hand, if you're in a niche that you truly care about and can envision yourself one day helping people on a more personal level - like offering personal coaching – then absolutely yes, you should publish under your own name.

Either way, there's no right or wrong answer. It just depends on your long-term business goals and what you're looking to gain from your business.

How Long Should My Book Be?

The primary reason people buy self-improvement and "how-to" books is to improve their lives in some way whether it's mastering a new skill or overcoming a challenge they're facing.

So as long as your book is well written and provides readers with the solutions to their problems, most people prefer a book to be shorter rather than longer.

Value isn't found in the number of pages but in the contents of those pages.

The reality is, people are busy and attentions spans are shorter than ever. No one wants to have to slog through 300 pages of garbley-gook when the same result can be achieved in 200 pages or less.

Books that are unnecessarily long can overwhelm readers and they will become frustrated if they aren't able to finish it.

Not only do they get upset with themselves for their failure to complete the book, but they often blame the author for being needlessly wordy and repetitious. *And rightly so.*

Worse yet, the promise of the book (which is the entire reason they purchased it in the first place) often gets lost and never fulfilled.

Readers are done with the fluff. They want short, concise books that make their points faster. This isn't just my opinion: it's fact.

Consider this: Blinkist.com is a professional book summary app that condenses non-fiction books into 15-minute key takeaways. They currently have 19 million users and are growing at a rapid rate.

Even best-selling author, James Patterson, has gotten in on the short book action. He recently launched a concept called Book Shots, where he dedicates an entire section of his business to short books under 150 pages and prices them under five dollars.

Readers aren't the only ones who benefit from shorter books. Self-publishers also benefit in several ways.

- Shorter books are less expensive to produc
- You can price your e-books between $2.99-$4.99 in the *"impulse buying zone"*.
- You can produce twice as many books. Multiple books boost visibility.
- It allows you to focus on one topic to help readers achieve a specific result.
- Shorter books are easier to write.

Ideal word count

I've found that right around 30,000-35,000 words is the sweet spot for most self-improvement books. It's long enough to give real value but short enough so readers don't lose interest.

The shorter the book, the more concise and value-packed the information needs to be.

One of my best-selling books was only 15,000 words. Readers loved it because it was jam-packed with valuable information and devoid of any fluff. They even left me comments saying even though the book was short; they were giving it five stars because the content was so good.

To give you an idea on book length, a 30,000-word book with a 6 x 9 trim size is roughly 80 to 110 pages, depending upon spacing, font size and graphics. If you use a 5.5 x 8.5 trim size, which is what I recommend, then your book would be roughly between 160 to 180 pages. For perspective, this book is approximately 28,500 words.

Formatting and Design

The interior layout and design of a book matter more than you think. Just because you're self-publishing doesn't mean your book should look like it's self-published.

An unprofessional-looking book can make you look like an amateur and may call into question the quality of the contents and your authority on the subject. If you want people to value the contents of your book, then it needs to look like it was written by a professional.

When it comes to formatting, avoid the temptation to purchase software and do it yourself. Here are a few reasons why I always outsource the formatting:

1. The process can be tedious and time-consuming, and that's even when you know what you're doing.
2. It's another skill you need to learn that will eat up a big chunk of your time and head space, and ultimately delay the publishing of your next book.
3. Successful business owners stay focused on money-making activities. The hours spent trying

to format a book could be spent on more critical business tasks. Keep your main thing the main thing; and your main thing should be publishing more books.

For a 30,000-word book, you can hire a good book formatting professional for around $40-$60 on Fiverr or Upwork. The cost will vary depending upon any images and graphics you want to add. No matter who you choose to work with, make sure to request the source file in case you need to make adjustments to your book the future.

Another affordable formatting option is to purchase pre-made templates. You can find a great selection of templates at BookDesignTemplates.com. The templates are compatible with Word or Pages so you won't need to buy any expensive software.

Module 5
From Idea to Published

I start with a solid outline so I always have those touch points that keep me on the path from A to Z." -Tom Clancy

In these next two chapters, you're going to learn how to get from the *idea* stage to being fully published, even if you have zero writing ability.

Don't let the notion that you need to be a writer prevent you from creating a wildly successful book business that enables you to serve others and make your contribution to the world.

Being an author does not necessitate you being a writer. The two are not mutually exclusive. The writer is the person who actually writes the book while the author is the one who originates the ideas for a book. Sometimes they are the same person, but in many cases, they are not.

Look at Tom Clancy or James Patterson, two of the most successful and prolific authors of all time. Have you ever wondered how they are able to publish so many books month after month?

Surprise. They don't write all their own novels. I apologize if I disappointed any Clancy or Patterson fans but the fact is, both authors outsource many of their books to ghostwriters.

Due to their overwhelming popularity, the demand for their books exceeds their capacity to write new ones. The fact that they outsource much of their work only proves that they're also great businessmen as well. They know that it's bad business to let a good book idea go to waste.

You might be asking yourself how these well-known authors are able to maintain consistency in the tone of the novels they outsource. *Great question.*

They begin by providing their ghostwriters a thorough and detailed outline. Then, throughout the entire writing process, they periodically review the ghostwriter's work to ensure it stays consistent with their overall vision for the book.

Once they receive the final draft back, they will make edits and revise where necessary. This is the same exact process I use with my ghostwriters and the one I recommend if you aren't planning on writing your own books.

Regardless of whether you decide to outsource or write the book yourself, organization and a clear plan for your book are essential for getting it written quickly, efficiently and in line with your overall vision.

owing five steps will help you to produce a high-
book quickly and efficiently.

Make sure you don't rush through or eliminate any of these steps; otherwise, you may risk wasting a lot of time and reducing the quality of your book.

Step 1. Research Your Topic

Now that you've chosen your book's niche and topic, it's time to get busy researching your book. If the topic is something you know a lot about, then this part should be a breeze.

But regardless of how much you know about the topic, you still need to do some research to ensure you produce a high-quality book that readers actually want to read.

Your first objective is to get an understanding of all the different ways that other books in the niche present and offer solutions for the topic.

Start by researching the top six to ten books surrounding your niche. It's not necessary for you to read each book in its entirety; you can just skim through the contents and focus on the major points.

As you do the research, ask yourself these questions to get a better understanding of your competition.

- How is the book structured?

- How are the chapters laid out?
- What is the tone and style of writing?
- How could the book have been better in your opinion?
- What did you like and dislike about certain books?
- How much fluff can be eliminated?
- What points did you agree and disagree with?
- What do customers say they liked or disliked about the books?

The answers to these questions will give you a deeper insight into your market. After reading all the different sides of an argument surrounding your topic, you'll begin developing your own unique point of view - one that's never been shared with the world before.

Make sure you record the location of any material that supports your ideas when doing your research-this way you or your ghostwriter can reference it during the writing stage.

Step 2. Brainstorm Chapter Ideas

Now that you've done your research, it's time to get your ideas on paper. Before the writing process even begins, do a brain dump of all the information that was gathered during the research phase.

Start by writing a rough list of what you feel are the main points and concepts for the book. At this stage, it's not necessary to put them in order. This isn't the time to organize. Expect things to be a bit chaotic at first.

Begin grouping the ideas you think belong together. Eventually, these groups will become your chapters and sections. The chapter titles don't need to be anything sexy yet; a basic description of what your chapter is about will do for now. Later on, you can go back and throw your magic spin on them.

Try to resist the temptation at this point to go down the rabbit hole by starting to write; otherwise, you may find yourself going down the wrong hole, especially if you haven't developed a hook for your book yet.

At this point, you should have at least a basic working title. A working title will help clarify your book's idea and keep you focused. It's okay if you haven't decided on your exact book title yet; it will probably evolve a few times before you settle on one.

Step 3. Create Your "Program" Steps

Now that all your ideas are out of your head and on paper, it's time to structure your outline. Having a detailed outline can save you hours of wasted time and effort when it comes time to write.

Think of your outline as your book's skeleton: its to hold the book's content in the correct place. functions as a roadmap to keep your writing from wandering off topic.

You wouldn't take a cross-country road trip without first punching in the coordinates in your GPS; or build your dream home without having a blueprint to follow.

The same rules apply to writing a book; your outline is your blueprint that will guide you every step of the way.

While the process for outlining a self-help or "*how to*" book is similar to other types of non-fiction books, there are some minor differences.

The good news is they are some of the easiest books to outline. Because topics focus on helping readers achieve a certain result, each chapter can be broken down into a stage or step in the process that you will *"teach"* to your ideal reader. The chapters will actually start writing themselves!

Start by breaking down the information into a certain number of steps or stages. Lay your book out like you would a system or program; for example, a 5-week program or a 7-step system. Make sure not to list too many steps. It should seem very *doable*.

Here is a template you can follow to help structure your self-help book outline for maximum impact.

The Introduction

- Let readers know that you understand their pain.
- Defines *who* your book is for (such as new moms looking to lose weight).
- Shows readers how your book is the solution to their problem.
- Assert your (or your ghostwriter's) experience or knowledge of the subject.
- Paint a picture of a brighter future that will be achieved by reading your book.

Chapter 1:

- Define the problem or the pain your reader is having.
- Introduce your unique solution.
- Explain why your solution is effective.
- Compare your methods to others and explain why your solution is superior.
- Share stories and real-life examples.
- Show how you or others were able to use these steps to overcome the problem or achieve your goal.

Chapters 2-12 (and beyond):

- Give readers the exact steps to achieve their goal.

- Each chapter is written as a step or stage in your process.

Step 4. Outline Each Chapter

The next step is to organize the content within each individual chapter. Not only will this keep you hyper-focused on the topic at hand but it also ensures the organizational flow of information is uniform throughout your book.

Here is a sample chapter outline:

Chapter X: [Your Chapter's Working Title]

- *Quote:* (optional) start with a chapter quote to set the tone for the chapter.
- *Chapter summary:* One or two sentences that explain what the chapter is about and why your readers need to know about it.
- *Create a list of supporting ideas*
    - supporting idea
    - supporting idea
    - supporting idea
- *Key takeaways (optional)*
    - key takeaway
    - key takeaway
- Transition to the next chapter (optional)

Step 5. Create Intriguing Chapter Titles

When naming your chapters, try to avoid making the titles too generic or boring. Craft them in a way that sparks curiosity and entices the reader to want to know more.

Intriguing chapter titles will not only "*hook*" readers and make them want to keep reading but they are also displayed in your table of contents (TOC). Most authors and self-publishers don't realize the significant impact that a TOC can have on book sales.

Whenever a potential customer lands on a book's product page, the first thing they do is click on the "Look Inside" feature to get a better idea of what the book's about. They do a quick scan of the TOC, the introduction, and the first chapter before making their decision to buy.

So, in essence your TOC functions as an extension of your sales page (more on this later). This means your chapter titles are actually a great marketing tool and definitely worth the added time and effort that you put into them.

Just be careful that you don't make your titles so clever that readers have absolutely no idea what the chapter is about.

Organizational Tools

Organizing and keeping track of all your research can get overwhelming pretty quickly. Fortunately, there are a few really great tools that can help.

Scrivener is a popular writing software that can make organizing and outlining your book a breeze.

I love the drag-and-drop function that allows you to move chapters and sections around very easily. And for those who prefer a more traditional method of outlining, Scrivener also has a "corkboard" feature that allows you to arrange all your research on "notecards."

One drawback to the software is that it can be somewhat challenging to master because of the many features it offers. So, unless you're a fulltime writer, you probably won't be able to take full advantage of all Scrivener's capabilities.

Another great tool for managing content is Evernote. Before Scrivener, Evernote was my go-to-app for outlining books. Although it's not specifically designed for book outlining, Evernote does offer some cool outline templates you can download.

You can also create your own book outline by creating a new "notebook" and saving it with the name of your book. Next, create individual "notes" within the notebook to house all your chapters.

It may not have all the functionality of Scrivener, but it's very simple to use and best of all, it's free!

Module 6
Expertly Outsourcing Your Book

"Do what you do best and outsource the rest."
- Peter Drucker

Typically, there are two ways to go about getting a book written. The first is to write it yourself. Keep in mind that if you're trying to publish a thirty-thousand word book every four to six weeks, you need to write a minimum of 1,000 words per day.

For most people, myself included, this isn't as easy as it sounds, especially if you're not in the habit of writing every single day.

The second option is to hire a high-end ghostwriter to write the book for you. This is how politicians and successful business people go about getting their books written.

But high-end ghostwriters don't come cheap. They can easily set you back anywhere from twenty-thousand to one hundred-thousand dollars. I'm guessing that's probably not a viable option for you either.

However, there is a third option for getting your book written that not many people talk about. It's how I'm able to get my books written within thirty days for $1,000 or less.

The Hybrid Ghostwriting Model

The hybrid ghosting model requires a little extra work on your end compared to a high-end ghostwriting service, but it's well worth the savings.

The main difference between the two is that high-end ghostwriters are usually deeply involved in their client's book writing process and the entire project can usually take up to six months to a year to complete.

That's because premium ghostwriters are involved in every aspect of the book production - from conducting multiple client interviews, researching, transcribing, book coaching, editing and proofreading - just to name a few.

With the hybrid model, the ghostwriter is less involved. Their overall level of involvement depends on how involved you want to be in the process. There are several ways you can go about this.

Outsource the research. If you're someone who truly enjoys writing, but hate doing fact-gathering, you could outsource the research and write the book yourself. This is typically how many big-name, non-fiction authors go about it.

Outsource certain chapters. For example, y‹ outsource chapters where the information proprietary and can be easily researched. This would dramatically speed up your book's production time.

Do the research yourself and outsource the writing. With this option, you would be responsible for doing your own research, creating a detailed outline and hiring a ghostwriter to write the book. This is the same process I normally follow.

When it comes to getting your book written, there isn't a *one-size-fits-all* solution. There are no rules when it comes to getting your book to the finish line. But whichever direction you decide to take, you'll need to find a talented ghostwriter or two to add to your team.

Where to find writers

You can find talented writers from all over the world on freelance platforms such as Upwork.com and Freelancer.com. About one-third of freelance writers are full-time. That means they spend their entire working days doing one thing – *writing.* Many full-time freelancers are able to deliver a thirty-thousand-word manuscript within just three-to-four weeks.

You might be wondering: *if these writers are so talented, then why don't they just publish their own books?*

In fact, many of them do.

However, the majority of writers lack the marketing skills to make their books successful. And many of them will openly admit they have no desire to learn marketing either. They simply love writing and are thrilled that they can get paid to do something they love.

It's a win-win scenario.

Finding a good ghostwriter

If you decide to publish your book under your own name, a major challenge you may face when working with a new ghostwriter is their ability to capture your "voice" or "tone".

You will probably need to adjust the first draft when you get it back so it sounds more like you. If you've chosen the right ghostwriter, it should be an easy fix. I always do quick edits and modify drafts, even on books published under pen names.

To save yourself the time and frustration of having to extensively edit your first draft, have your writer send you the first chapter before going any further. This way you can see whether or not they're even capable of capturing your voice. If not, you may want to pass on them and go with a different writer.

It's also a good idea to inject some of your own personal stories and experiences into your book where appropriate to really make it your own. It will help to establish your authority on the subject and increase readers' trust.

If you have limited or no experience on your topic, then ideally you should hire a ghostwriter who does. Try to find one who has actual real-life experience in your niche and not just experience writing on the topic.

For example, if you're in the real estate niche and your topic is rental properties, the ideal ghostwriter will have actual experience as a landlord. If your ghostwriter is an expert on the topic, and you're writing under a pen name, then you can let them use their own voice and stories.

Inform your ghostwriter up front that you're writing a series of books, and if all goes well, you would be interested in contracting them to write your other books.

A multiple-book contract is very appealing to writers because they won't have to waste time searching for other writing gigs. And more importantly, you'll be able to keep the tone and voice of all your books congruent.

Hiring your ghostwriter

One of the most popular websites for hiring freelance writers is Upwork. Just about anyone who has ever hired a virtual assistant or freelancer before is familiar with the platform. It also happens to be my preferred website for hiring writers.

A major benefit of hiring on Upwork is that they manage the contract side of the transaction. The funds are held in escrow between the two parties and are only disbursed once the contract is fulfilled. This helps keep both parties safe.

With approximately 1.5 million freelancer writers on the platform, you can find some truly amazing talent. By the same token, you will also find many freelancers who will exaggerate their writing abilities or outright fake their credentials.

The biggest challenge you'll face finding your ideal ghostwriter is being able to identify the good writers from the bad.

Or as my granny used to say, "*You need to separate the wheat from the chaffe, sweetie.*"

Before you even consider hiring a writer, you need to do your due diligence *first.* It will save you *tons* of time and untold frustration.

Vetting Your Ghostwriter on Upwork

- *Carefully read the applicant's bio.* A freelancer's bio is your first look at the potential candidate's writing ability. If the profile has spelling and grammatical errors or is awkwardly written, it should be an automatic hard pass.

- *Read previous client reviews.* Always read the reviews left by previous clients. You can learn a lot about a freelancer's work ethic from what previous clients had to say. This is the equivalent of an employer checking on an applicant's past employment record.

- *Review the freelancer's portfolio.* Take the time to carefully review all writing samples provided within a freelancer's portfolio. If the work they are showcasing is full of spelling and grammatical errors or displays amateur-level writing, you can be assured that the work they submit to you will be dramatically worse.

- *Job success score.* Only hire applicants with a job success score of 90% or above. The job success score measures a freelancer's contract history, client relationships, and any feedback. Occasionally, you'll find good writers with lower scores, but it's usually the exception, not the rule. If you don't filter applicants by their success score, your inbox will be flooded with subpar writers that require more of your time to vet.

- *Hours billed.* Look for freelancers who have earned at least $10K and above. This demonstrates that a freelancer is consistent and has a solid track record. It will also help you avoid the *"here today, gone tomorrow"* freelancers. That said, there are some legitimately good writers who may be new to Upwork. In that case, base your decision on the quality of their past projects which were done outside the platform (in addition to the other criteria mentioned here).

- *Writing samples.* The best candidates will have personal experience or knowledge in your niche. When writing your job description, ask the freelancer to describe their actual experience and include any writing samples related to the topic.

- *Conduct a video chat interview.* Request to do a video chat interview with potential candidates. This way, you can confirm that they are who they say they are. You can also verify that they are a native English speaker. If a freelancer refuses or has an excuse not to do the video interview, it should instantly set off alarm bells.

Sample job post on Upwork

- **Job Title:** *Ghostwriter needed to write a 25-30K word book in the [NICHE] niche*
- **Job Category:** *Ghostwriter, Writer*

- **Job Description:** *Choose "ongoing" (if creating a series of books)*
- **Skills Required:** *eBook, non-fiction, eBook writing, fact-checking, content writing, ghostwriting, research, English grammar, book writing*
- **Scope of Work:** *Medium (well-defined project)*
- **Length of Time:** *1-3 months*
- **Level of Experience:** *Intermediate*
- **Location:** *Worldwide*
- **Maximum Project Budget:** *$750-$1000 (start low, you can always increase your bid)*
- **Screening Questions:**
    - *Do you have real-life experience in the X (niche)? Please explain.*
    - *How long will it take to complete this project?*
    - *What's your experience writing books with 30K+ word count?*
    - *Do you have pending projects that must be completed prior to starting this project?*
- **Advanced Preferences:**
    - *English Level: Native*
    - *Number of professionals needed: 1-3*
    - *Hours Billed on Upwork: At least 100 hours*
    - *Job Success Score: 90% job success and up*
    - *Rising Talent: Yes*
    - *English Level: Native*

Job Preferences:

- Only Upwork users
- Cover letter? Yes

Job Description:

Our company is looking to hire a talented ghostwriter to write a series of books in the "X" niche. The right candidate will ideally have actual experience in the "X" niche so that he or she can better understand the reader's problem or pain. Candidate must:

- Write 30k words in the "X" niche.
- Write a unique, 100% original high-quality book.
- Must be a native English speaker.
- Perform an in-depth research on the topic.
- Write engaging and conversational content.
- Deliver grammatically correct content, free of spelling errors.
- All content must be free of copyright violations.

Please submit 1 to 3 sentences explaining why you feel you are a good fit for this position. You must be able to deliver the completed project within 3-4 weeks of the hire date. The book outline and table of contents will be provided by us.

Please apply with your proposed rates for this project and any sample of your writing pertaining to this niche. We are happy to potentially negotiate our rates for the right person.

Inviting freelancers

Upwork allows you to invite up to 30 freelancers to your job post. Make sure to take advantage of these invites. The most talented writers will have built up solid reputations and have repeat customers; this means they most likely won't be closely monitoring the open jobs board searching for writing gigs.

Limit the candidates you invite to only those who closely match your criteria. It will increase the likelihood that they will reply to your invite.

Module 7

Strategic Keyword and Category Optimization

"Cultivate visibility because attention is currency." -Chris Brogan

Many authors and self-publishers believe they need to find thousands of readers to get their book on the bestseller's lists. But that's the exact opposite of how it actually works on Amazon. You don't need to find your readers. Your readers need to be able to find *you*.

As you currently read these pages, your target audience is frantically scouring the Amazon bookstore searching for the solution that your book can solve. Your job is to make sure your book is placed directly in their path.

Proper keyword selection and category optimization are the holy grail when it comes to exposing your book to a hungry audience.

Finding keywords that convert

In order for your book to be discovered by your ideal readers, you need to know which keywords they are typing into the Amazon search bar. The process of keyword selection is very similar to how you would search for your niche as discussed back in Module 2.

1. Make sure you are using "incognito" mode on your Google browser.
2. On the Amazon search bar, choose either "books or "kindle store".

3. Begin typing your keyword until Amazon auto-fills it, and shows you suggestions just below the search box.

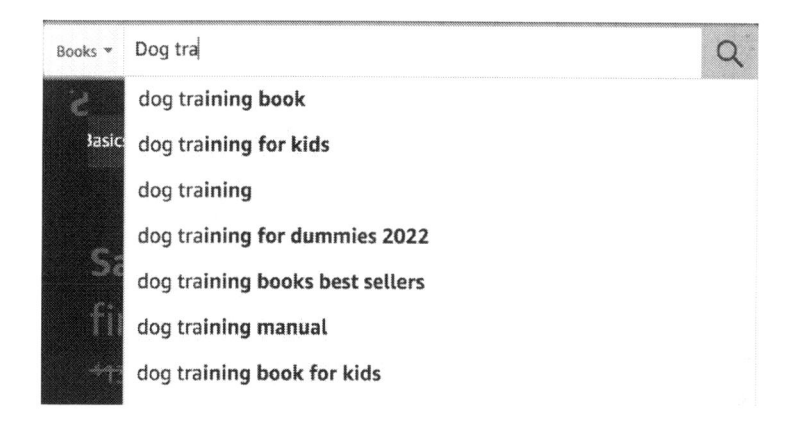

4. Keep adding different letters of the alphabet one at a time to the end of the phrase to see how Amazon auto-completes it.
5. Write down all of Amazon's keyword suggestions.

Examining keyword data

Although the auto-complete feature is very effective at helping you generate targeted keywords, it does nothing to determine the search volume or competitiveness of each keyword.

For this, you will need a special tool. The software I recommend is *Publisher Rocket*. It will give you the hard data you need for choosing the best keywords.

- It helps to easily identify the competitiveness of certain keywords, the total number of Amazon searches, and the monthly average earnings for the top books in your niche.

- It gives longer keyword variations for short keyword phrases. As discussed, longer keywords are less competitive.

- It analyzes and scores the competition level. The competition score is a number between 1 to 100; this tells you how hard it would be to rank for a certain keyword.

There can be hundreds, if not thousands of keywords in your niche so it's crucial to choose the ones that not only have the most search volume, but you actually have a chance of ranking for.

Choosing your "Big Seven"

When you first upload your book to the KDP platform, you are given seven boxes with which to enter your targeted keywords.

For each box, you are allowed up to 50 characters to enter a single keyword or targeted phrase. This is an area where many self-publishers go wrong. They don't optimize these keyword boxes to the fullest capacity and miss out on some prime digital real estate.

Enter up to 7 search keywords that describe your book. How do I choose keywords?

Your Keywords (Optional)

dog training	obedience, logbook, journal, manual
dog training for kids	german shepherd, guide, games
dog training for beginners	rescue dogs, for dummies, puppy
e-collar, for puppies, behavior solutions	

I've also made some big mistakes in this area which has probably cost me thousands of dollars over the years. But when I made a few minor adjustments to *how* I entered my keywords, I saw a significant increase in book sales.

Take advantage of the 50-character limit

Amazon allows you to enter keywords and phrases into each box up to 50 characters long. Research has shown that Amazon will rearrange the words in every combination; the more phrases and keywords you enter into the box, the more keywords your book will be indexed for.

Since Amazon does seem to give an extra boost to exact match phrases, I recommend using one to three boxes for your most relevant, exact match keyword phrases. Fill the remainder of your boxes with as many relevant keywords and phrases as you can so you utilize as many characters as possible.

Since it's difficult to fill a 50-character box with one keyword or phrase, choose one very relevant keyword or phrase, then fill in the remaining characters with other relevant keywords. It's not necessary to use any word more than once.

Use your best keywords in your book title

Make sure your best, most relevant keywords can be found in the title or subtitle of your book since Amazon gives them the most weight. Amazon also recommends not to reuse the same keywords that are in your title for your backend keywords.

You won't be penalized if you do repeat a keyword, but it won't help your book rank any better, and you could end up wasting a keyword box.

Never use quotations

Using quotation marks around your keyword phrases will prevent Amazon from indexing for different combinations and variations of your keywords.

Targeted phrases are more effective

Generally, the shorter the keyword phrase, the more competitive and harder it is to rank for. Longer keyword phrases will not only help you directly target your ideal audience, but they make it much easier to rank your book.

For example, *Dog Training* is a much more competitive keyword than *Dog Training for Beginners,* which is much more targeted.

Keywords to Avoid (according to Amazon)

- Subjective claims about how great your book is
- Obvious descriptive words (like "book" or "eBook")
- Time-sensitive, descriptive words like "new" or "on sale for a limited time"
- Intentionally misspelled words and some slang words
- Anything that could be deemed as misrepresentative
- Amazon program names like "KDP" or "Kindle Direct"

- Various versions of pluralization, capitalization, punctuation, or spacing

Category Bestseller Secrets

The Amazon categories you choose for your book will have a direct impact on your chances of becoming an Amazon bestseller. Many self-publishers get a little lazy when it comes to good category selection. Or perhaps they don't really understand the impact it has on a book's visibility.

The good news is that their oversight opens up a huge competitive advantage for you to gain major traction with your book.

As discussed in the previous chapter, Amazon assigns books a BSR (best sellers rank) based on how many books have sold within a certain period compared to other books that sold. The lower the BSR, the higher the volume of books sold. Conversely, the higher the BSR, the lower the volume of books sold.

Now here's where it gets really interesting. Amazon has over 14,000 categories and subcategories, each with their own Top 100 Best Seller list. Plus, new categories are being added all the time. The more categories there are, the better your odds are of becoming a bestseller.

There's a good chance your book will probably fit into a number of different categories, so it makes sense to choose ones where your book has the best chance of becoming a bestseller.

For example, if you were to choose a less competitive category where the #1 book had a BSR of 50,000, your book would need a BSR of 49,999 to become #1 in that category.

Best Sellers in Caregiving Health Services

#1	#2	#3
CCM Certification Study Guide 2022-2023:... Matthew Bowling ★★★★☆ 37 Paperback $32.99 **#173,841** in Books (Top 100) ASIN: 1516721152 Sold by Amazon	The Dementia Concept Joshua J. Freitas ★★★★☆ 45 Paperback $16.82 **#466,800** in Books (Top 100) ASIN: 0692447350 Sold by Amazon	Palliative Care Perspectives James L. Hallenbeck ★★★★☆ 2 Paperback $42.50 **#640,886** in Books (Top 100) ASIN: 0197542913 Sold by Amazon

It's a heck of a lot easier to become a bestseller in that scenario than if you chose a more competitive category where the top-ranking book has a BSR of 10,000 or below.

There are a couple of ways to go about finding less competitive categories. The first way is to drill down to the furthest subcategory on the category string as possible.

To get an idea how this works, go to Amazon's book store or Kindle department and scroll through the left sidebar until you see the list of book categories.

When you click on a category, a list of subcategories will appear. When you click on a subcategory, more subcategories will be displayed.

Keep clicking until no more new subcategories are offered. That's when you know you reached the end of the category string.

Kindle Store > Kindle eBooks > Crafts, Hobbies & Home > Antiques & Collectibles > Art

When you list your book in a deep subcategory like this, Amazon automatically lists your book for all the parent categories. So not only do you benefit from having your book listed in a main category, but it shows up in several subcategories as well.

So, what are the benefits of being ranked #1 in a category?

Amazon slaps the *"bestseller"* tag above your book. The bright orange badge not only grabs a lot of attention but it helps persuade readers that your book is worth a closer look. The badge offers further social proof that your book is a good purchase.

How To Get Your Book Listed in More Categories

When you first publish your book on the KDP platform, you are only able to submit your book to two categories. Most self-publishers are unaware that once a book goes live, Amazon allows you to add your book to eight more categories.

The more categories your book shows up in, the more opportunities you have to get your book noticed. It makes absolutely no sense not to take advantage of this extra exposure.

You will need to reach out to KDP support by email to get your book added to more categories. It can take up to two days so make sure you contact support as soon as your book goes live.

How to contact KDP Support:

1. Log in to your KDP account.
2. Go to your Author Central page.
3. Click "Help" on the top navigation bar.
4. Then click on "Contact Us" on the bottom right. Under "How Can We Help", select "Amazon Book Page".
5. Next, click "Update Amazon categories".

In the e-mail box provided, politely ask to have your book added to additional categories.

Make sure to include the full category string as shown in the following example:

"Hello,

Could you please add my book (Your Title & ASIN#) to the categories below?

Books > Business & Money > Management & Leadership > Training

Kindle Store > Kindle eBooks > Business & Money > Management & Leadership > Management > Management Skills

Thank you!"

Category strings for paperback books are different from Kindle eBooks, so you will need to provide both.

Pro Tip: If you are adding multiple categories, send two separate email requests, one for Kindle eBooks and one for paperbacks. It keeps things from getting confusing.

Advanced Category Strategies

When choosing categories, it's important to choose the ones that will give you the most bang for your buck. The best strategy is to use a mix of categories that have a low, medium, and high range of competitiveness.

Here are some guidelines to follow when choosing your categories:

1. **Low Competition.** Choose a few categories where it's easy for your book to rank number one. Search for categories where the #1 book has a BSR above 40,000 or 50,000. The higher the BSR, the easier it will be for your book to become a bestseller. Just make sure the category is relevant to your book.

2. **Medium Competition.** Choose a few categories that have medium competition, where the top 10 books have BSRs under 50,000. These are the main categories that will bring you consistent sales.

3. **High Competition.** Choose one or two high competition categories where the top 10 books have BSR's under 20,000. These categories can give you high visibility, especially during your launch phase.

This process of finding and analyzing categories can be very time-consuming and tedious to do manually. This is another area where the Publisher Rocket software can drastically reduce research time.

Module 8

Building A Raving Fan Base

"Loyal customers, they don't just come back, they don't simply recommend you, they insist that their friends do business with you as well." - Chip R. Bell

Your loyal fan base is the backbone of your entire business. The main reason why so many self-publishers fail to make a significant income is because they haven't taken the time to build a loyal following.

Loyal fans are repeat customers. It's much easier to sell to someone who has purchased from you in the past than to someone who has no clue who you are. Not to mention cheaper advertising costs.

Your fan base will happily refer your books to others while continuously buying from you again and again. They are also a key factor when it comes to getting reviews for your books.

Without a loyal list of readers who are eager to buy and refer your books, you'll be forced to rely heavily on paid marketing. It's an expensive and potentially risky position to be in. Should any competitors in your niche have a deeper funnel (multiple books and products) than you and a higher lifetime customer value, they will easily be able to outbid you for your main keywords.

Without repeat buyers or a reliable source of advertising, your book will quickly fade from the charts (assuming you were able to get there in the first place) and you'll be forced to start from scratch every time you launch a new book.

Don't make the fatal assumption that you need to wait until your book is published before beginning to build your fan base, otherwise you'll miss out on a huge window of opportunity that comes in the early stages of your book.

The best time to start building your fan base is right now, *before* your book is published. This will help you get those first reviews and downloads that are critical to getting your book off to a strong start.

Building a raving fan base doesn't have to be complicated. It can be accomplished in 5 easy steps:

Step #1. Track the un-trackable

One of the biggest drawbacks to publishing on platforms like Amazon is not having access to customer contact data once the sale is made. That's because technically, they aren't your customers. They belong to Amazon.

If you want to achieve stability in your business, you need a way to reach out to readers and build relationships with them. The best way to accomplish this is by building a customer e-mail list.

Don't make the mistake of thinking that a social media following is the equivalent of having an e-mail list. It's not. Unlike your Facebook, YouTube, or Instagram followers, you actually own your customer e-mail list. This is of critical importance to your business.

Social media sites are always changing their rules. One day you're in compliance, and the next day you're not. If you're not paying attention, you can wind up losing access to your entire audience. It happens all the time.

When you rely heavily on social media websites to house your fan base, you risk losing an audience that you spent years building, all to the whims of a new social media algorithm.

That's *not* to say you shouldn't grow your social media presence (if you have the time), but your first priority should always be growing your e-mail list.

Main benefits of having an email list:

- Helps kick off your book launches.
- Helps sell more books. Happy readers are repeat buyers.
- Makes your business much more valuable if you ever decide to sell it.

- It's an asset you own.
- Allows you to offer other goods and services to readers.
- Allows you to build long-lasting relationships with customers.
- It's an effective, low-cost marketing option.

There are many good email providers that you can choose. GetResponse, AWeber, Convertkit, Mailerlite, and Mailchimp are all good options.

But if you're just getting started and on a tight budget, Mailerlite and Mailchimp are both good options. They are both free for up to one-thousand subscribers. The interfaces are drag and drop, which makes creating opt-in forms and landing pages a breeze.

As your email list grows, you may want at some point in the future to move to a more robust provider; but for now, these are great low-cost solutions.

Step #2. Create A Compelling Lead Magnet

A lead magnet is an important component for building a fan base and bringing readers into your author ecosystem. Lead magnets are resources you give away for free via e-mail in return for a reader signing up for your e-mail list.

An effective lead magnet is the solution for taking an untrackable Amazon customer and converting them into your own customer.

The best place to offer a lead magnet is in the front or back of your book. This encourages your most interested readers to join your mailing list while they are still actively engaged with your book.

There are a variety of different lead magnets you can offer, but the most effective will usually have the following essential features:

- **Related to your book's topic.** Your lead magnet should be closely related to the problem being solved in your book.
- **Quick to consume**. The best lead magnets are short, sweet, and to the point. The last thing you want is to overwhelm your readers.
- **High perceived value (and actual value)**. It's okay to hype your lead magnet as long as it provides real value. Delivering an over-hyped, low-quality lead magnet is a fast way to lose the trust of your readers.
- **Problem —> solution specific.** Good lead magnets pinpoint a specific problem and provide a specific solution.
- **Delivers a quick win.** Your lead magnet should help readers quickly achieve something or solve a

specific problem, without overwhelming them in the process.

- **Instant access.** Your lead magnet needs to be deliverable immediately. People want instant gratification.

One of the best ways to find great ideas for your lead magnet is to see what the competition is doing. Do a quick search of the top books in your niche and browse the first few pages. Good marketers will usually have their lead magnets prominently displayed in the front of their books.

This doesn't mean you should ever copy or plagiarize anyone's work. Only use them as a means to inspire ideas and concepts for your own lead magnet. Here are the seven best-converting lead magnet ideas:

A. **Checklists.** Checklists are probably the easiest of all lead magnets to create. They're easy to consume and usually convert very well. Readers love when things are condensed into actionable lists.

B. **Cheat sheets.** Cheat sheets are similar to checklists, except they list a set of guidelines or an exact process that can be followed to achieve a certain result. You can easily go through your book and organize the main points into a sequence of steps. People appreciate cheat sheets because they can make the process easier to implement.

C. **Swipe Files.** Swipe files are a collection of done-for-you marketing templates that a reader can easily copy and make their own. For example, you can create templates from your top-performing e-mail campaign, complete with subject lines and body text. Swipe files are personally one of my favorite lead magnets to download.

D. **Video Tutorial.** A video tutorial is another popular lead magnet to offer that enables you to explain a specific process or strategy in more depth. Try to choose a specific stage in the process that will be easier to understand with visual presentation. Keep the video short (under 10 minutes) so it's easily consumable.

E. **Toolkit.** Toolkits are a list of tools and other resources that you or others are currently using to achieve great results. Everyone wants to know which tools successful people are using. To make your list even more irresistible, include as many free tools as possible. The word "free" makes for a compelling headline.

F. **E-books** The most successful ebook lead magnets will be very specific to your topic. It's not necessary for your ebook to be lengthy; in fact, shorter ones are preferable. Shoot for around 10 to 15 pages. The content should be easily consumable and focus on solving just one problem related to the book topic.

G. **Planner/Calendar** A planner or calendar is a dated itinerary that helps your audience implement a plan of action. People love knowing exactly what to do and how it should be done. One of my best lead magnets was a beautifully-made planner that cost me around $25 dollars to have made on Fiverr.

Step #3. Set Up Your Launch Team

Getting some early reviews for your book following its release is a crucial first step in starting to convert potential readers into paying customers.

One of the first things most readers do when they land on a listing is to read the reviews. If your book has zero reviews, your target audience won't see your book as a credible source. Without social proof that your book is a good purchase, most readers won't take the risk.

If you're launching your first book in a series (which I'm assuming you are) and you don't have a large e-mail list or following on social media (which I'm assuming you don't), I highly recommend that you assemble a launch team.

A launch team, also known as ARC team, is a group of readers who will support your launch by helping you get the initial reviews for your book.

ARC stands for *advanced reader copy*. An ARC is an early copy of your book that is given to a select group of people about two weeks before its release date.

This select group is known as an ARC team. The goal of creating an ARC team is to ensure that your book receives reviews within the first few days of its release. The number of reviews received is usually influenced by the size of your team and the frequency of your communication with them.

Creating Your ARC Team

Assembling an ARC team doesn't have to be complicated. There are a few websites that will help you create and distribute your ARC links to simplify the entire process.

The website I recommend is Booksprout. Not only does Booksprout enable you to create a special link where people can download a copy of your book, but they also have a large network of built-in readers who are ready to download your book and leave a review.

In addition, Bookprout automatically sends reminder emails to pre-readers letting them know that their review is due soon. This saves you the time and effort of doing it manually.

It's important to give pre-readers at least two weeks to read your book before scheduling its release date. This way, your ARC team will be ready to post their reviews when your book goes live.

Set a goal to give away a minimum of 50 ARC downloads. Don't expect everyone who promises to leave you a review to follow through. People get busy and stuff happens. That's just the way it is.

The more ARC's you can give away, the better. It's better to overshoot your goal than underestimate it. This way, the worst that can happen is you end up with more reviews.

On average, you can expect anywhere from 5 to 10 people from within Booksprout's network to download your book. That number will go up or down, depending on the popularity of your book topic.

The balance of your ARC links will need to be downloaded from other sources. The best place to find more ARC readers is on social media sites.

- Start by making a post on any Facebook or other social media platforms where you're active and ask if anyone would appreciate an advanced copy of your book.
- Join ten Facebook groups specific to your book's topic. Choose groups that have at least 1,000 members and appear to have a lot of activity. Once you're accepted into the group, start

- interacting with other members and posting valuable, helpful content.
- Once you have established a presence in the community, post that you've recently written a book on your topic and you really welcome member feedback. Don't ever just spam groups with your request or the group admins will likely reward you with an instant ban.
- When members respond positively to your request, contact them privately via Facebook Messenger with the details and a link to your ARC. The more authentically you approach social media with your request, the better response you will get.

Many people, and you may be one of them, hate doing direct social media outreach. But it's a necessary step to make sure your book gets off to a strong start until you grow your own audience.

Pro Tip: Once your book is live, don't forget to remove it from Booksprout otherwise, if your book is enrolled in KDP Select, it could violate Amazon's terms and conditions

Step #4. Run Book Promotions

Book promotion websites are extremely powerful tools for launching a book and building a fan base quickly.

They are a fast and easy way to get your book in front of your ideal readers.

These sites have thousands of avid book readers on their mailing lists, all hungry for discounted books. That's why many promo sites will only accept your book if it's being offered for free or at a steep discount.

Many authors tend to get squeamish at the idea of giving away their book for free. But the benefits are more than worth it. A high-quality promo site can get you hundreds of downloads and sales, which will have a major impact on your Amazon rankings - especially during your launch phase.

Once your book goes live on Amazon, scheduling your book promotion is a very simple process. Just submit your book's details (book title, book description, author name, ASIN, etc.), choose the date you want to run the promotion, and the site will blast your book to their reader base.

Some of the higher-quality promotional sites will require your book to have between 5 to 10 reviews before they will accept it. These initial review requirements are often a huge roadblock for many newbie self-publishers. But if you set up your ARC team as discussed and follow the *launch strategy* as outlined in the next module; you'll have no problem meeting the review requirement.

Free Promotions Vs Paid

Primarily, there are two kinds of promotions you can run: a free book promotion and a paid book promotion. To clarify, a free book promotion refers to promotions where you're offering your book for free by enrolling it in KDP Select. It doesn't necessarily mean that the cost to promote your book is free-although it can be.

Paid book promotions refer to promotions where your book is being offered at a steep discount, usually at $0.99 cents. Many promo sites will offer both free and paid promotion options.

The most effective approach to using these promo sites is to "*stack*" them. "*Stacking*" refers to running several different promotions over a short period of time, usually 7 to 14 days.

The goal of stacking is to make sure your book gets a steady stream of downloads and sales within the first two weeks. This is your one shot to impress Amazon and you don't want to blow it by having inconsistent or short spikes in book sales.

It's also important to stack your promos from least effective to most effective so that your book sales are trending in an upward trajectory. Amazon favors books that show sales are increasing over time.

This book promotion strategy greatly increases the probability that Amazon will continue to promote your book beyond the 30-day launch window. This is a key component to organically ranking for your keywords.

Recommended book promo sites

There are literally hundreds of book promotion websites to choose from. Some better than others. Prices can range anywhere from *free* to over $500 dollars per promotion. The average cost for the ones I typically use are between $25 to $35.

The list below are my recommended promotion sites for when your book is on *free* promotion:

- RobinReads (www.robinreads.com)
- The Fussy Librarian (www.thefussylibrarian.com
- Free Booksy (www.writtenwordmedia.com)
- Book Doggy (www.bookdoggy.com)
- RealUrbanEmpire (www.fiverr.com/realurbanempire)

The following list are promo sites *(listed according to their effectiveness)* for when a book is discounted to $0.99 cents.

Good

- Awesome Gang (www.awesomegang.com)
- Just Kindle Books (www.justkindlebooks.com)
- It's Write Now (www.itswritenow.com)

- Bookbongo (www.bookbongo.com)
- Snicklist (www.snickslist.com)
- Book Doggie (www.bookdoggy.com
- BestBookMonkey (www.bestbookmonkey.com)
- BKNights (www.fiverr.com/bknights)

Very Good

- Awesome Book Promotion (www.awesomebookpromotion.com)
- The Fussy Librarian (www.thefussylibrarian.com
- ManyBooks (www.manybooks.net)
- Free Kindle Books & Tips (www.fkbt.com)
- My Book Cave (www.mybookcave.com)
- eReader Café (www.theereadercafe.com)
- Digital Books Today (www.digitalbooktoday.com)
- Booksends (www.booksends.com)
- Book Runes (www.bookrunes.com)
- Book Lemur (www.booklemur.com)

Best

- Book Bub (www.bookbub.com) (very expensive but very powerful and not recommended for first time launch)
- Bargain Booksy (www.bargainbooksy.com)
- Book Gorilla (www.bookgorilla.com)
- Buck Books (www.buckbooks.net)
- EreaderNewsToday (www.ereadernewstoday.com)

- EReaderIQ (www.ereaderiq.com)
- Robin Reads (www.robinreads.com)
- Bookdealio (www.bookdealio.com)

I've personally used many of the promotional sites on this list at one time or another, while a few others have come highly recommended to me.

It's a good idea to keep a back-up list of promotional sites in case your *"go to"* sites are booked out too far in advance.

Step #5. Create a Killer Author Bio

While creating an author bio isn't the most critical step to growing a fan base, it's not one that should be overlooked either.

Your Amazon author bio is the very first opportunity to brand yourself and connect with your potential readers. If you don't take the time to create your author bio, you could be leaving a lot of money on the table.

Usually when a reader is debating whether or not to purchase a book, they will click through to the author page to see if you are *"legit."* This is your first chance to begin building trust and credibility.

Your author page also lists all your other published books. So, if a reader likes one book, there's a good chance they will click to see what other books you've written. This is another easy way to inexpensively drive sales to your other books.

Writing your bio

Keep your bio short and to the point. The ideal length is one or two paragraphs. Try to keep your word count less than 150 words max. The first few sentences of a bio are a great place to include a *call to action* that directs readers how to find out more about you. This is the ideal place to include a link to your website or your landing page.

If you don't have a website yet, you can direct readers to your social media sites. The more breadcrumbs you leave behind, the greater chance you'll have of drawing readers into your author ecosystem.

While it's important to include any relevant experience or achievements in your bio, try not to go overboard. Only include what's relevant and necessary for credibility. It may sound counterintuitive, but your bio isn't really about you; it's about what your reader stands to gain by reading your books.

Many gurus will advise you to write your bio in the third person. While it's certainly less awkward, I personally don't feel it matters one way or the other as long as it's written professionally.

Most readers are savvy enough to recognize that most author bios are written by the author themselves and not by some big-name publishing company.

What to include

Your Author Mission Statement

Express who you are, what kind of books you write, who you write for, and why.

Credibility

Share your experience and expertise in your niche if you have any. This can include other books you have written.

Personality

Let readers know that you are a real person. You can do that by sharing some of your hobbies or interests. You can also do it by the words you use to express yourself.

A Call to Action

Direct readers what to do next. For example, to get notified of my upcoming books, sign up for my newsletter at www.mywebsite.com.

Your "website" can just be a landing page where readers can sign up for your lead magnet.

Setting Up Your Amazon Author Account

- Go to www.author.amazon.com.
- Log in with your KDP credentials.

- Enter the author name for your books.
- Under the profile tab, upload your author photo, bio, and create your custom author page URL.
- Under the books tab, claim any books that are yours. If any of your books don't show, you can search for it by title or ISBN.

Amazon allows you to add up to seven different pen names per Author Central account. The first three you can set up on your own. To activate the remaining four, you will need to reach out to KDP support.

Module 9
The 6-Figure Launch Blueprint

"Marketing begins before the product is launched." -Seth Godin

Why Your Launch is Crucial

Your launch strategy will affect your sales in both the short and long term, and, ultimately, determine your overall success. I cannot emphasize the importance of a good book launch. It can be the literal difference between your book earning $100 dollars per month vs $1,000 dollars per month.

When you launch your book both powerfully and strategically, you're able to take full advantage of Amazon's algorithm. Not only will it help solidify your book's organic ranking, but it will also reduce the need to spend big bucks on advertising later on.

One of the main reasons many authors struggle to get book sales is because they think their job ends after they push the *"publish"* button. They adopt the *Field of*

Dreams strategy. They think just because they build it, readers will come. But the reality is *this*: no matter how well written your book is or how good the information is, no one is going to buy it if they don't know it exists.

The good news is that Amazon highly favors newly released books. In fact, it's during the launch phase (the 30-day period that immediately follows your book release) that you have the greatest chance of your book reaching best seller status.

During this time, Amazon will temporarily boost your ranking by giving your book an artificially low BSR which gives your book more exposure. Experienced publishers often refer to this as the *"honeymoon stage."*

But after that, the rest is up to you.

If your book shows a consistent upward trend in sales over the next 30 days, you can solidify your organic ranking in Amazon once the launch is over. It's also possible Amazon may continue promoting your book after the initial launch period has ended, sometimes for as long as sixty days.

If your book continues to convert well and make sales beyond the launch, Amazon may begin recommending your book to their e-mail list and other places on their website. This is how you successfully *"ride the Amazon algorithm"* as they say, and should be the goal of all your launches.

On the flip side, if your book shows a lack of sales or displays short, inconsistent sales spikes within the first thirty days, Amazon will stop promoting it, and your organic ranking will fall quickly. This is what some self-publishers refer to as the *"the dead cat bounce",* and as the name indicates, is something you want to avoid.

If you don't have a launch strategy in place that plays well with Amazon's algorithm, it's highly unlikely that the book will do well long term. It's essential to prove to Amazon that your book is worthy of promotion by generating a constant stream of sales during the thirty-day launch phase.

My Step-by-Step Launch Blueprint

In this next section, I'm going to share with you the exact launch strategy I personally implement to launch my books to bestseller status and get them organically ranked for my keywords.

Before you begin this prelaunch phase, make sure the following steps are completed:

- The final draft and layout of your ebook and print book are formatted and proofread.
- The book covers for both your ebook and print version are ready to upload.
- Your author e-mail account and e-mail list are set up.

- Your lead magnet has been created and a link has been inserted in the front of the book.

Phase One: Pre-launch
(30-days before launch)

Step 1: Decide the exact day your book will go live. Make sure to give yourself a minimum 20-day buffer window. This allows for a couple extra days in case things don't go as expected.

Keep in mind that it can take anywhere from 24 to 72 hours for your book to go live on Amazon once you hit the publish button. If this is your first time publishing, it can take a minimum of 36-hours, so plan accordingly.

Step 2: Schedule your ARC (advanced readers copy) on Booksprout at least 14-days prior to your scheduled launch day. This two-week period is necessary to make sure your launch team has enough time to read your book before posting any reviews.

Step 3: Reach out to your e-mail list (if you have one) and any social platforms and share your ARC link with any potential pre-readers.

Step 4: Join ten Facebook groups related to your topic. Start interacting with the group members and sharing value. Post a request asking any members if they would be interested in giving feedback on your new book.

Phase Two: Launch Week
(Days 1 through 14)

Step 5: Upload your ebook and print draft to KDP at least two days before your official scheduled launch date. Remember, it can take 24 to 72 hours for your book to go live.

Step 6: Price your ebook at $.99 cents and make sure your paperback is competitively priced for your niche.

Step 7: As soon as your book goes live, submit your book's ASIN# to Booksprout. An auto-reminder will be sent to your launch team to post their honest reviews.

Step 8: Reach out to anyone else who has received an advanced copy and remind them that it's time to leave their review. Don't forget to provide your ARC team with a direct link to your review page.

Step 9: Immediately schedule your book for one of the *free* book promotion websites listed in the previous module. Remember, good promo sites get booked out quickly so make sure to do this right away.

Step 10: Enroll your book in KDP Select.

Step 11: As soon as you secure a date with the book promotion website, schedule your book for a *free* promotion in KDP Select. Run the promotion for three to five days. Make sure the date coincides with the date scheduled with the book promotion website.

Step 12: Once your book has at least 5 reviews, schedule your *"paid"* promo sites. Make sure your book is priced at $.99 cents. Try to schedule one promotion every day for twelve days if you can afford it. Otherwise schedule for as long as your budget allows. Don't forget to schedule promotions from weakest to strongest.

Step 13: Send an email to your email list (if you have one), letting them know that your book is live and they can purchase it at a discount.

Step 14: Begin running Amazon Ads. (If you're unfamiliar with how Amazon ads work, there is a free training in my Facebook group: www.facebook.com/groups/onebookaway

Phase Three: Post-Launch
(Days 15 through 30)

Step 16: When all book promos have ended, raise your ebook price to $3.99 or $4.99 (the impulse zone.)

Step 17: Continue raising your paperback price until you see the profit start to dip.

Step 18: Start researching keywords for your next book.

Step 19: Rinse and repeat the book creation and launch process for your next books. The launch can seem a bit complicated at first, but it gets easier with your 2nd, 3rd and 4th books.

If you go through all the trouble of writing a quality book, and you took the time to give it a good title and book cover, then you can't afford not to give your book the launch it deserves.

By investing your time and money into doing a proper book launch, you are giving your book the greatest chance of having long-term success.

Plus, you won't need to rely as heavily on paid marketing in the future to keep your book profitable. These early-on marketing strategies combined with a loyal audience will do most of the heavy lifting.

Keeping Sales Flowing

Now that you know how to create and launch your books like an expert, you need a good post-marketing plan to keep the momentum going. Without a post-launch marketing strategy, your book will slowly begin to drop in rankings, and your sales will start to slow.

Fortunately, there are a few simple but powerful marketing strategies you can implement to help keep your book ranking high and your sales flowing in. One highly effective but often overlooked method is to periodically discount your books while running ads or paid promotions to them.

Not only will it drive sales to the book you're promoting, but it also drives sales to all the other books within your book funnel.

Remember, nothing sells your first book like your second book. But in this case, nothing sells your first book like your third, fourth or fifth book.

As an added bonus, this strategy also helps to exponentially grow your mailing list.

The net effect is a powerful marketing wheel, where each book perpetually drives sales to the other books in your funnel, while also helping you to grow a massive fan base.

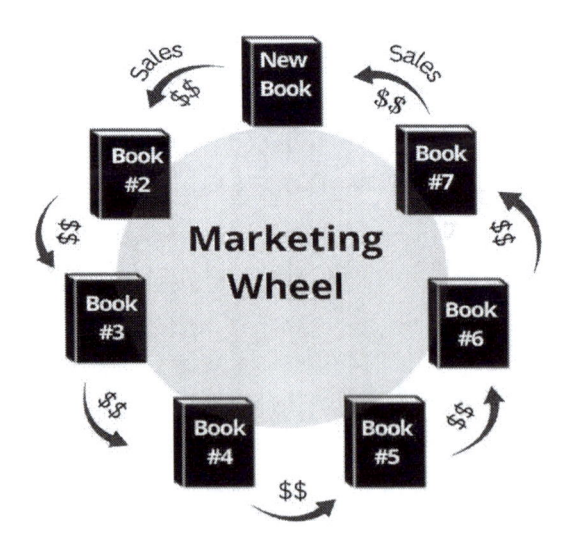

To execute this strategy, your book needs to be enrolled in KDP Select to be eligible to run Kindle Countdown deals.

A Kindle Countdown Deal allows you temporarily discount an ebook to $0.99 cents while still retaining a 70% royalty rate. Usually, books priced below $2.99 have a 35% royalty rate.

This is *huge!* The higher royalty helps you recover the cost of your book promotions much faster. In most cases, you are able to recoup the bulk of your promotion expenses within the first week.

More importantly, it increases your chances of getting your book back on the best seller list.

Post-Marketing Strategy

- Run a Kindle Countdown promotion on your books every 90 days.
- Set your price to $.99 cents throughout the entire promotion.
- Schedule the promotion to run for 5 to 7 days.
- Run paid promotions to your book the same way you would with your initial book launch (with the exception of running free promotions).
- Keep a calendar for when your books become eligible to run a Kindle Countdown deal so you don't forget.

- Rinse & Repeat.

Keep in mind that while you're promoting older books on the backend using Kindle Countdown deals, you're also launching new books on the front end that are being heavily promoted by both you and Amazon.

This results in a wave of visibility and sales that flows in from the front, middle, and back of your book funnel.

The Power of a Perma-Free Book

As your portfolio of books begins to grow, you can turbocharge your results by creating a permanently free book on Amazon that can hook thousands of new eyeballs and drive even more visibility and sales to your other books.

A perma-free book doesn't need to be a full-length book. You can create a 7,500 to 10,000-word book that is specifically designated to attract new readers to your brand. You always have the option to turn it into a paid book at a later day.

Some self-publishers balk at the idea of giving away a book for free that could potentially be bringing in sales. That's a short-term thinking mindset and a large part of why so many self-publishers fail to earn a significant income.

If your goal is to quit your job and create long-term passive income, then you need to play the long game when it comes to building your business.

When you use perma-free books as part of your overall marketing strategy, you'll see firsthand the backend benefits far outweigh any upfront losses.

Module 10
Adding Additional Revenue Streams

"The moment you make passive income and portfolio income, your life will change." -Robert Kiyosaki

Now that you have successfully published and launched your first book, it's time to look at the different ways you can add additional income streams from your existing books *without* having to publish new ones. Some call this repurposing content. Others call it double-dipping. But whatever you want to call it, what could be better than taking one source of your work and turning it to multiple streams of income?

Book Bundle Magic

One of the easiest ways to add additional revenue streams is with book bundles. Book bundles, also known as boxsets, are when you combine two or more books into one which creates an entirely new product that you can sell on Amazon.

You can create many different combinations. For example, you can create a two-bundle book *and a* three-bundle *and a* four-bundle book. How many you combine is totally up to you. Although Amazon doesn't limit how many times a book can be included in a bundle, they do caution you not to abuse the process.

Not only do bundles allow you to produce multiple products, but you're able to sell them at a higher price point than single books, but they essentially cost nothing to produce. In addition, readers love bundles because they're able to purchase multiple books at a steep discount. And in many cases, bundles sell just as well if not better than single books.

Bundling is not just limited to ebooks either. You can bundle paperbacks and audiobooks as well. This opens up a multitude of income streams that can be created from your existing assets, all with very little added expense.

If you're wondering if creating boxsets will negatively affect the sales of your individual books, the answer is *not at all*.

When taken as a whole, the extra royalties earned by selling boxsets far outweighs what you may lose on individual sales. If anything, the discount you offer on boxsets can convince readers who have been sitting on the fence to finally pull the trigger.

That said, I recommend waiting at least 30 to 60 days after launching your book before putting it in a bundle, to avoid undermining the success of your launch.

How to Create Your Bundle or Boxset

The best part is that you don't need any fancy software to create bundles. You can do it right in Microsoft Word by following these steps.

1. Create a new book title for your bundle" (Ex: Urban Garden Mastery: 3 Books in One).
2. Combine all the books into a new Word document.
3. Create a new title page
4. Leave a blank page in between each book to separate them.
5. Delete the table of contents from each book.
6. Create a new Table of Contents (include all the title chapter headings from each book).
7. Create a new book description that includes information from each book.
8. Have a new 3D Boxset ebook cover and paperback cover created at Fiverr.com.
9. Launch your boxset in the same way you would a new release.

Pro Tip: *A great place to offer your bundle is on the "Thank You" page when people sign up for your mailing list. Instead of having a generic thank you page, you can direct readers to your bundle page.*

It's another easy way to increase sales without spending money on advertising.

Profiting with Series Pages

Another way you can increase revenue is with Amazon's series pages. A series page is a separate product page created by Amazon whenever two or more books share the same series name. It acts as a kind of dedicated landing for the purpose of highlighting a book series.

There is even a "Buy Now" button that allows readers to purchase the complete series, which can significantly increase your royalties.

Once you publish your second book in the same niche, you have unofficially created your first series. To make it official, all you need to do is link the books together by assigning them the same series name from within your KDP dashboard.

Series pages can majorly affect your bottom line because:

- Readers can purchase the entire series with one click.
- There are no ads on series pages, so you won't have to compete with other books or products.
- Amazon personalizes the "buy button" for each reader and will not include books they already own.
- Amazon lists all your books together in a row on your book description page similar to the *"also bought"* page.

Series Page Requirements:

- You must have at least two books.
- Books must share the same series name.
- The name in the series field must match exactly on all books.
- All books must be written by the same author.
- The series name must appear in one of these locations: the book cover, the book interior or the book description.
- The books must be available for purchase.

Once your books meet these requirements, Amazon will automatically create a series page for you. You also have the ability to create a series page from your KDP dashboard.

Doubling Your Income with Audiobooks

With the hard part of creating and launching your book behind you, it's time to start thinking about creating your audiobook. Audiobooks present you with another opportunity to create a brand new revenue stream that can potentially blow up your sales.

If you don't take the time to create audio versions of your books, you are literally leaving money on the table.

Audiobooks are a billion-dollar industry that continues to increase its market share every year, not that it should come as a surprise. Most people these days simply don't have the luxury of sitting down for hours to read a book and prefer to multi-task.

It's much easier to listen to a book while doing other things like exercising, cooking, cleaning, or driving home from work. If you don't have an audiobook version, you will be missing out on a very large segment of the market.

In many instances, audiobooks actually outperform print books and ebooks combined. And because of the low production cost to create an audiobook, your ROI (return on investment) can be infinite.

Creating Your Audiobook

Creating your audiobook may sound intimidating, but it's actually very easy to do. Amazon's audiobook distribution platform, called ACX (Audiobook Creation Exchange), makes it super simple to hire narrators and get your files uploaded. To get started, go to ACX.com and use your KDP credentials to log in. Once your account is set up, locate your book by typing in your book title or ASIN number.

After agreeing to ACX's terms of service and filling out the book's details, you will be able to choose from thousands of narrators. To narrow down your search, you can filter by things like language, price, and male or female voice.

Once you've finished posting the details, you will start to receive auditions from narrators who meet your parameters. The applicants will forward a brief excerpt read directly from your book.

The narrator you ultimately choose should ideally have a voice that is congruent with the subject of your book. For example, if your book is for teen girls, you may want to choose a female narrator with a young-sounding voice. Or if your book targets senior citizens, you may want to choose someone with an older voice.

Criteria to consider:

- Voice and tone: narrator voices come in all shapes and sizes: young, old, upbeat, depressing, overly dramatic, or too robotic. Choose the one you feel is most congruent with your book.
- Pace: some narrators read too slowly, and some read way too fast. However, pace is something the narrator has a degree of control over. Before disqualifying someone based on narration speed, ask them to send you another sample at your desired pace.
- Sound quality: audio quality is extremely important. It's very easy to tell which narrators use quality equipment and which don't. Any auditions you receive, where you detect background noise or it sounds like they are

recording in a long hallway or tunnel, should be quickly eliminated.

Pricing Your Audiobooks

Unlike KDP, ACX doesn't allow you to set the price of your audiobook. The price is automatically determined by the length of the audio.

Below are the current minimum pricing requirements:

- Under 1 hour: $3.95
- 1-3 hours: $6.95
- 3-5 hours: $14.95
- 5-10 hours: $19.95
- 10–20 hours: $24.95
- Over 20 hours: $29.95

On average, it takes a narrator approximately one hour to narrate 10,000 words, depending upon how fast or slowly they speak. Therefore, narration time for a 30,000-word book is around 3-hours.

To give you an example, a recent book I turned into an audiobook contained 27,500 words. Because the narrator spoke on the slow side, the finished narration time was 3 hours and 6 minutes.

If the finished audio had come back just seven minutes shorter, I would have missed out on the next pricing tier, which is a significant chunk of change to lose for only a few minutes of audio. That's why it's important to make it clear to your narrator up front that your audiobook needs to be a minimum of three hours.

Experienced narrators are able to tell you with almost precise accuracy how long it will take to narrate your book. And if necessary, they will adjust their narration speed to accommodate you.

The cost for narration is normally charged by "PFH", which means *price per finished hour*. That means you only pay for the finished length of the audio, not how long it takes for the narrator to record it.

The per finished hour rate I recommend is $50 to $70 PFH. There's really no need to pay more. Narration is a very competitive market, and you will find that the level of talent and professionalism available at that price point is really very good.

The average cost for me to have a three-hour book narrated is between $150 to $210. Most times I'm able to recover the production costs within two to three months. All royalties from that point forward are pure profit; almost infinite.

Promoting Your Audiobooks

A major difference between ACX and KDP, is that ACX allows friends and family members to leave reviews. Not only do they permit it, but they actually encourage it by giving you up to 50 free promo codes per marketplace (Audible U.S. and Audible U.K.).

Audio promo codes are like coupons that allow people to redeem your book for free. It makes getting those initial reviews for your audiobook that much easier.

To be eligible for promo codes, your audiobook will need to be exclusive to Audible. After one year, you can email ACX and request to end your audiobook's exclusivity if you decide you want to put it on other platforms.

The best ways to share promo codes:

- Give them to friends and family members
- Post on your Facebook page and groups
- Make an announcement to your email list
- Swap with other self-publishers
- Join audiobook promotion sites like AudiobookBoom.com and AudioFreebies.com

Currently, the ACX platform is available to people living in the United States, the United Kingdom, Canada and, more recently, Ireland.

Module 11
Selling Your Business For Multiple 6-Figures

"Spend time upfront to invest in systems and processes to make long-term growth sustainable." - Jeff Platt

Planning Your Exit Strategy

Throughout this book we've discussed the different strategies and benefits of growing a passive income publishing business. But there's still one very important factor to consider as you scale your business.

What will your business be worth if you ever decide to sell it?

It may not be something you've given a lot of thought to at this point. The last thing that's probably on your mind right now is selling a business you haven't even created yet.

But what if I told you that within the next twelve months, it's very possible your book business could be worth multiple six-figures?

And what if I told you that at the time of writing this book, business brokers like EmpireFlippers.com are currently valuing book businesses at 35 times to 45 times their monthly net income, some of the highest multipliers to date?

Apparently, it seems that a passive income business is highly desirable to investors. *Who would have known?*

Regardless of what your long-term exit strategy is, it's always good to know what your business is worth at any given time.

Here are some current valuations based on your monthly net revenue if you were to sell your publishing business today:

Monthly Net Income Sales Price

$1000	$35,000-$45000
$1500	$52,000-67,5000
$2500	$87,500-$112,000
$5000	$175,000-$225,000
$10,000	$350,000-$450,000

Isn't it exciting to know that a business that generates just $5,000 per month could potentially be worth multiple 6-figures?

Now that you understand that building a self-publishing business has real marketability and appeal to outside investors, does it change your perception of how you view this opportunity? *It did for me.*

When I first began publishing books years ago, it never occurred to me that I may actually want to sell my business one day. To be perfectly honest, I didn't even know it was possible to transfer a KDP account.

My primary goal was always to create a business strictly for the passive income and financial freedom it could provide. If I knew then what I know now, I probably would have done a few things differently.

For starters, now whenever I make any business decisions, I factor in how they will affect the long-term marketability and not just the immediate benefits.

By approaching it this way, you're less tempted to cut corners or be lazy when it comes to building out your brand or growing your email list - because now you understand those things have <u>real</u> monetary value.

It's also comforting to know that, should the necessity or desire ever arise to sell, your business is fully optimized to sell for top dollar.

The irony is, that when you build a business with the intention of selling it one day, you ultimately end up with a business that's more profitable, diversified, and stable should you decide to keep it.

Factors That Determine Business Value

- **Monthly Net Profit** The total net profit after all expenses (advertising costs, ghostwriters fees, paid promotions, tools, etc.).

- **Number of Books in Your Portfolio** More specifically, the number of books in your portfolio that are earning royalties. A business where all royalties are coming from just one book is much riskier and less desirable than a business with royalties spread over multiple books and formats.

- **Diversified Revenue** Income that is generated from multiple sources such as affiliate income, AdSense from blogs or YouTube, or companion courses makes a business highly desirable.

- **Established Brand** Having an established brand that serves one niche. Ideally, all your book covers are branded and share a unified theme, making them easily recognizable. Your author profiles have a blog or active social media accounts.

- **Systems and Automation** The more hands-off a business is, the more desirable it is to a buyer. A business that automates and systemizes the day-to-day tasks using automation tools, trained team members, and SOP's (standard operating procedures) will sell much faster and for more money.

- **Email Lists** The size and response rate of your email list has a direct impact on business valuation. Having an automated email sequence set up to deliver emails for months in advance is also recommended.

When is the Best Time to Sell?

The only person who can determine the best time to sell is *you*. There may come a time in your life when you find it necessary to liquidate your business for personal reasons or to take advantage of another business opportunity.

Either way, it's not a decision that you should take lightly, especially if your business provides your main source of income. There are also the tax ramifications to take into consideration.

If your sole reason to sell is just to *"cash out"*, and you don't have any plans for reinvesting the money, it's probably wise to wait until you have a solid financial plan in place.

If, however, you have other income sources and you plan to reinvest the proceeds into another asset, selling your business could make more financial sense.

For example, you could decide to invest your proceeds in real estate - the ultimate wealth builder - or pay off your home mortgage. You may want to invest in cryptocurrency or the stock market. All these things could further support your goal of financial wealth and freedom.

The good news is that selling your book business doesn't have to be the end. *In fact*, it could be just the beginning. Once your KDP account is sold and transferred out of your name, Amazon allows you to open a new account. This means you're free to build another business all over again.

You could even make *building and selling* a part of your overall business strategy. Except, you'll be far more knowledgeable and experienced the second and third times around, enabling you to scale your business much faster and more efficiently.

There are a number of possibilities and directions you can go with your book business. All you need to do is get started!

Did You Enjoy This Book?

Thank you so much for taking the time to read this book! I sincerely hope you found value in it on your quest to financial freedom.

Before you go, I have one small favor to ask. If this book has inspired or helped you in some way, could you please take a moment to leave a review?

Someone could be searching for this information right now and a few words from you can make all the difference. You never know whose life your words could impact!

Plus, hearing from you would really make my day!

-Gracie

Scan the QR code with your phone camera to leave a review

References

[1]. Ovens, Sam "Why you should eat your customers complexity" YouTube video, 21:42. July 17 2018
https://www.youtube.com/watch?v=16JwTEUtoA8

[2]. Quicksprout, November 19, 2014 Quicksprout.com "How to Get 247% More People to Read Your Content"
https://www.quicksprout.com/how-to-get-247-more-people-to-read-your-content/

Printed in Great Britain
by Amazon